ADRIAN STALHAM

C000180142

THE FUTURE BUSINESS FORMULA

How to change faster and accelerate business success

FOREWORD BY MIKA HÄKKINEN,
FORMULA 1 WORLD CHAMPION 1998 AND 1999

R^ethink

First published in Great Britain in 2023
by Rethink Press (www.rethinkpress.com)

Cover image © Shutterstock | Yauheni Meshcharakou

Illustrations by Virpi Oinonen | Businessillustrator.com

Contents

Preface

Back in 2019, I had the privilege of watching Mark Gallagher speak about 'business transformation in the fast lane', using the evolution of the Formula 1™ industry as the metaphor. Mark's insights and stories from the world of Formula 1 racing were not only informative, but also captivating – in that room filled with 150 senior business executives, I saw a level of engagement that I had never witnessed before.

After the keynote, many of the attendees and clients all had one question: how could they apply the strategies Mark spoke about in Formula 1 to their own business to transform at speed? I truly believe the transformation the Formula 1 industry has gone through is the closest comparator to what the business world is and has to go through.

That's when I had a vision. I wanted to bring Mark together with Adrian Stalham, Sullivan & Stanley's Chief Change Officer, to create a fundamental guide on the future of business. I knew that by combining Mark's expertise in high-performing Formula 1 teams and his Performance Insights business with Adrian and Sullivan & Stanley's knowledge of business transformation consulting, we could create something special.

And so the journey began. With the support of Sullivan & Stanley and Performance Insights, Adrian and Mark have worked tirelessly to distil their collective experience into 12 critical principles that any organisation can use to thrive in a complex and fast-changing world.

The ambition for this book is to do for the world of business what *The Agile Manifesto* has done for software development. So, if you're looking to take your business to the next level, I am confident *The Future Business Formula* will inspire you, challenge you and help you change faster and accelerate your business success.

Pat Lynes
Founder and CEO, Sullivan & Stanley

Foreword

Formula 1 is a business, a global sports business, and one in which success depends on team leaders who have the ability to tackle relentless challenges directly. Change is ever-present, it is an accepted part of the Formula 1 ecosystem and we know that to be competitive, to win, you have to focus on building a team which can see the opportunity in change.

Like many industries, Formula 1 is highly regulated yet somehow we have to constantly innovate. It also involves a great deal of technology, and while it is in our nature to want the latest, greatest technology, we also know that there are many other considerations. For me, as a driver and the end user of the car, I need to have confidence in the technology being safe and reliable as well as high-performing.

While the regulations and technologies are always changing, we also operate in a highly competitive environment in which our very smart competitors are trying to find ways to jump ahead of us. Standing still is not an option. We must keep on measuring our performance, using every opportunity to learn, and to ensure a winning performance can be sustained.

The only way to be able to achieve true success in such a fast-moving business is to have the best possible team, talent and culture. A team that is fully aligned behind the strategy, working and collaborating in the best way possible, looking at the data and making smart, high-quality decisions.

The McLaren team with which I won the Formula 1 World Championship in 1998 and 1999 was like this. Well led, with a big ambition, it was a fantastic group of people who developed brilliant, innovative cars with which we could beat the competition.

From my own personal perspective, it meant focusing on the things that really mattered, prioritising the work which I did inside the team, helping my teammates to solve problems and to always keep progressing.

What I really like about Formula 1 is that successes and failures are public, there is no room to hide. The decisions we make every day, every week and every month make a difference, particularly when we have to show how good we are every two weeks from March to November.

I am happy to have been invited to write the Foreword for *The Future Business Formula* because I know, from my own personal experience, that many of the things we do in Formula 1 translate well into business. It is a brilliant sport to work in, highly complex yet dependent on people to be led and work together in a certain way.

I am sure that the lessons which Mark Gallagher and Adrian Stalham have developed, based on the twelve key principles shared in this book, will help the reader consider how to make sure their own organisation has the ingredients necessary to unlock sustained success. In a fast-changing world, every business leader needs the best possible help and support.

Mika Häkkinen,
Formula 1 World Champion

Introduction

Adaptability is critical

The future is no longer an extrapolation of the past. If you want to survive in business and remain relevant, then the ability to adapt quickly and effectively is critical to keeping your organisation alive, let alone thriving. More so now than ever before, change and transformation need to be a constant, an inbuilt capability, not just an exceptional one-time stop/ start activity. The dynamics of doing business in the twenty-first century have exposed how the management principles, practices and approaches designed for a previous era are no longer appropriate. The underlying formula for what makes a business successful has changed.

In this book, we explore how that success formula has transformed to suit the modern age and how you can apply it to future-proof your organisation. Inherent in this book is the need for organisations to be able to constantly change and improve, to evolve and self-heal. Change must become a fundamental attribute of every department, team, process and individual. We must shift the way we think about, and do, change, moving from an activity focus (sporadic, turbulent, when needed) to a capability focus (continual, normalised, inherent). The reassuring news is that our 'Future Business Formula', a new way of thinking about how to create success in organisations, is built from the ground up to be adaptive, resilient and embrace the complexity of the business world today.

The Fourth Industrial Revolution

The attitudes, behaviours and mentality that have kept organisations alive during a period of relative calm no longer work. We are in a world of hyper-volatility, hyper-connectedness and hyper-disruption following the shift from the industrial age into a knowledge age.

The industrial age relied on machines as the primary value-creation solution. Frederick W. Taylor (1856–1915) published his key work in 1911, *The Principles of Scientific Management*.[1] Taylor proposed dividing the organisation into thinkers (management) and doers (workers) and started the modern concept of management as a specialism and controlling mechanism.

He introduced the functional division of labour to the shop floor and performance management. Hierarchies and bureaucracy were created to drive maximum efficiency. Work and organisations were arranged in logical ways, dividing the work into activities and encouraging a mechanistic view of the world that meant everything could be planned and predicted. It revolutionised productivity during the time in history when workers left agriculture and cottage industries for factories where standardised work was king. Many of Taylor's approaches appear almost inhumane today. Yet his legacy remains incredibly strong as the principles and practices he created are still seen in most organisations over 100 years later.

The knowledge age started around the 1980s and is now in full flow. The globalisation of markets has created increased pressure alongside rapid technology improvements and increasing connectedness. There has been a fundamental shift in the overarching business model. Humans are now the primary source of problem-solving and value creation again. Our organisations are set up to deal with a complicated (industrial) world, just as the world became more complex. The saying 'what got you here won't get you there' has never been more accurate.

Why we wrote this book

According to Harter, in his Gallup Workplace article 'Historic drop in employee engagement follows record rise', 54% of workers are 'not engaged' – they are psychologically unattached to their work and their company.[2] These employees put time into their work, but not energy or passion, simply showing up and contributing the minimum effort required. Yet Sorensen states, in her article 'How employee engagement drives growth', that organisations with high employee engagement in the top quartile out-performed bottom-quartile organisations by 10% on customer ratings, 22% on profitability and 21% on productivity.[3] Disengaged employees cost US companies $450–550 billion a year in lost productivity. Business is in real trouble. Organisations are struggling, employees feel that work is a dehumanised environment with which they are not engaged and organisations' ability to change is severely compromised in this hyper-volatile world.

The 'Agile Manifesto' was written in 2001 and revolutionised the world of software development.[4] Many of the values and principles quoted in the manifesto are relevant for business as a whole, not just software development, but the manifesto has never been well accepted by the wider business world. Maybe its origin in the technology space has prevented much expansion beyond IT, but some companies and industries have intuitively used similar business-focused practices to become high-performing.

We wrote this book because we believe there is a better way of doing things. We use our experience and approaches to help organisations move in the right direction. We have consolidated that knowledge into twelve principles which we call the 'Future Business Formula' to help organisations focus on the right things in the right ways to win in an increasingly tough environment.

Adrian Stalham has spent many years nurturing change and transformation across different industries and passionately believes that a new approach to change is required for the modern world. Mark Gallagher provides companies with the opportunity to learn from the fast-paced business environment of Formula 1 motor racing and has delivered his insights to more than 800 companies spanning a diverse range of industrial and business sectors. The solutions that we talk about are born out of real-world experiences and come from decades of experience at the forefront of transformation in some of the biggest brands around the world. That experience has also identified what doesn't work. Change and transformation are difficult and success is rare, but we believe that implementing the Future Business Formula will give organisations a far greater chance of radically changing to become future-proof.

We have aligned our model with Formula 1 because it is the best example of how these principles, applied in a real-world environment, can drive success. Those stories come first-hand from co-author Mark Gallagher, a former executive from the world of Formula 1, having held senior positions with Jordan, Red Bull and Cosworth. Formula 1 is a highly regulated industry that has gone through radical change due to its external environment. It's a sector where change is constant – whether for regulatory, technological or economic reasons – and high-performance teamwork is inherent in accepting and exploiting the opportunities triggered by change. It remains a highly fluid, adaptive industry based on modern leadership, incredibly high performance, innovation, business agility and amazing collaboration. That's why it best exemplifies the Future Business Formula. Who wouldn't want to be able to change, transform and deliver like a Formula 1 team?

Who is this book for?

A key theme in this book is that of the punk or pirate mentality – the people within an organisation who are willing to challenge the status quo and are comfortable exploring the unknown and taking risks. We believe it is these punks, pirates, mavericks and rebels, the ones who see things differently, who are critical to the future of business.

This book is for people who are dissatisfied with the status quo, who consider themselves to be change activists, or who believe there is a better way of doing things. It is for the non-conformists – those who are brave enough to leave the well-trodden path, find their own way and forge a new trail.

Change as a constant

According to consulting firm Korn Ferry, the average tenure of an executive in a business has been reducing since 2016 yet, in our experience, the average duration of a traditional major project or a transformation programme has been growing.[5] As a consequence, transformation is often avoided rather than embraced because, by the time it is delivered, the executive has left the organisation. It's difficult to achieve engagement where the benefit is deferred to the long term.

The democratisation of technology means the barriers to entry in most industries are low. Change cannot be a long-term exercise anymore. Businesses have to develop the capability to break change down into small components so that it can be delivered constantly. Transformation traditionally has a start and an end point. At the end point, teams think the transformation is complete and they can relax. You have to constantly reinvent and transform and you can't do that using the methods that have served you previously. You have to rethink how it's done and transform through the line. This means introducing the principle of value delivered regularly (at least every ninety days for organisational change). We can no longer tolerate mega projects with promises of 'jam tomorrow' and plans lasting years. If you can find ways to deliver value every ninety days, those executives with a two-to-three-year lifespan will start embracing transformation because that value allows them to be successful in the short term, rather than having to wait for something to deliver in the long term.

The Future Business Formula

If we want our organisations to be future-proof, we need to change. We need to unlearn the business principles and practices of the past. They served us well during the Industrial Revolution and the following decades, but today we are seeing them stifle progress, adaptability and speed. If you want to be a future business, you need to reassess what you do, how you think, how you deliver and how you work. Being in business and being efficient are no longer enough. You need to be in the business of constantly improving your business.

The good news is that there is a wealth of useful knowledge and practice to experiment with. To experiment, we need to unlearn the way we think business should be done. Experience and intuition (we could call it our mindset) are incredibly valuable, but they can stop us from changing. Our experience is only based on things we have done before and therefore assume to be true in every context, and our intuition is a belief system that we rarely challenge. Both can be spectacularly wrong and keep you locked into your existing knowledge space. We need to find a way to allow external knowledge to challenge our mindset and thus find new solutions. Some people have this natural growth mindset and others are incredibly resistant to it. This book will resonate with the former and probably frustrate the latter.

We believe that twelve principles are needed for success. Twelve principles that address the key components of organisations. The reality is change is needed and fast. Time is running out. The pace of change and disruption is accelerating.

TWELVE PRINCIPLES	
Strategy	Create a strategy for an unpredictable world – emergent, adaptive, relevant.
Customer	Create experiences, the new differentiator.
Alignment	Embrace purpose and transparency, make action irresistible.
Leadership	Use influence to benefit others.
Culture	Be intentional about creating a positive culture.
Talent	Create the sought-after organisation to work in and work with.
Innovation	Leverage cognitive diversity; allow ideas to flourish.
Change and delivery	Focus on delivering small packets of value regularly.
Simplification	Operate at the speed of a start-up.
Organisational design	Embed an adaptive operating model.
Learning	Bring diverse opinions into the room.
Measurement	Measure what matters to the customer.

When put together, this twelve-principle Future Business Formula gives your organisation a chance. A chance to adapt, evolve and ultimately thrive in a world that is becoming more complex. A chance to energise your employees, giving them purpose and autonomy. A chance to delight your customers.

PART 1
WHAT WE DO

Our first three principles can be summed up as strategy. Strategy in its current form needs to change. Strategy with a big 'S' used to be the reserve of stuffy executives and suited consultants, creating corporate documents and plans that were rigid and based around a year that normally ended in a 0 or a 5. Strategy with a small 's' (business, data, technology, etc) was often overlooked or the realm of tactical responses. Rarely was the wider organisation engaged in the process or the ambition. The separation of thinkers/planners from doers was an artefact from the Industrial Revolution that outstayed its welcome. In the past, customers were mostly passive, accepting the experience and products they were presented with by companies. In a simpler, slower-paced world where scarcity was the underlying theme, this may have been sufficient.

The business world has speeded up. We are in an age of abundance. Five or ten years ahead suddenly became far-sighted horizons for strategies. Disruption appeared overnight for some industries and the gap between strategy and execution widened. New digitally native competition appeared that didn't play by your business model. Customers got connected to the internet, and with each other, and suddenly a world of information and experiences opened up. Employees started to search for a sense of purpose and self-actualisation at a younger age.

Strategy has to evolve to reflect a faster-paced world, with high levels of competition and digitisation and a workforce that wants more than just a job. It needs to accommodate ever-changing and fickle customer expectations. It must outpace and outmanoeuvre the competition.

Many organisations have failed in this transition. Many more will fail over the coming years. Working out what to do (and what not to), being truly customer-centric and engaging the workforce behind a vision are critical parts of the formula to becoming a future business.

In this first section of *The Future Business Formula*, we will look at our first three principles:

- An adaptive **strategy**

- Truly focusing on the **customer**

- **Alignment** through the organisation

1

Principle 1 – Strategy: For An Unpredictable World – Emergent, Adaptive, Relevant

Pit Stop – McLaren race strategy

Neil Martin, former Director of Strategy of the Scuderia Ferrari Formula 1 team, has held similar roles at both Red Bull Racing and McLaren. To maintain leadership in their field, top Formula 1 teams have to learn how to deliver significant value race-by-race, every seven-to-fourteen days. This demands iterative development and performance improvement.

Martin introduced real-time analytics to help Grand Prix teams develop the agility necessary to adapt strategies in response to a wide range of factors inside and outside of their control. From competitor behaviour to track evolution, tyre performance to fast-changing weather patterns – variables which can be planned for and strategised accordingly.

In an interview for this book, Martin said that his decision to work in Formula 1 was driven by a simple realisation: 'F1 is a true meritocracy where the organisation that does the best job generally wins. It is those who understand the need to be more effective in multiple areas that generate the competitive edge.'[6]

When Martin first joined McLaren, he found an organisation which had access to considerable data but did not understand the potential to mine that information in a way that would speed up decision-making and improve outcomes.

Martin cites an early example of a breakthrough in using data analytics to model potential strategies. This occurred after a major regulation change in 2003, when his team ran a huge number of simulations and identified that the right strategy at the first race in Melbourne would be to do something strange – namely, to make a pit stop with both cars right at the start of the race.

One factor that heavily influenced the modelling was the large number of rookie drivers that year. There was a high probability that one of them would make a mistake or have an accident, meaning that safety car periods were likely. This prompted Martin's model to suggest an early pit stop, ready to take advantage of the chaos that would ensue. This did not seem to be sensible and, when Martin's boss asked him to present the strategy to McLaren's CEO Ron Dennis, Martin recalls that the response was 'You won't be doing that with our cars!'

'As things turned out, we qualified mid-field and the management realised we needed to implement an innovative strategy,' explains Martin, 'so I deployed my model, asking David Coulthard to make a pit stop on the formation lap and Kimi Räikkönen to make a pit stop on lap three. They finished first and third, the latter because Kimi incurred a time penalty. The take-away is that when you combine the power of analytics with decision-makers who are experts in their field, you generate a rich outcome.'

When it comes to complex decision-making in business, Martin passionately believes that interrogating your business more deeply will help to unlock solutions to even the most daunting challenges. He warns that if you do not understand a subject area fully, natural biases will enter the decision-making, skewing the outcome.

Effective risk management is essential in Formula 1 where bad decisions can lead to catastrophic failures. Martin explains that it is precisely because leading teams are so good at managing risk that they can unlock new levels of performance within their strategies.

The world is now VUCA

In a volatile and unpredictable world, how many organisations persist with traditional approaches to strategy? Strategies that were pitched five years into the future, as if something unique is going to happen to the company in that magical timespan.

The paths to get there are pre-determined years in advance. Simple, linear timelines offer reassurance that events can be preordained, chaos can be managed, and success can be plotted and guaranteed.

Life, let alone business, simply doesn't work like that. In reality, our long-term plans largely fail because the future is uncertain; we live in volatile, uncertain, complex and ambiguous (VUCA) times. The more volatile the world is, the more and the faster things change.

Business dynamics have shifted too and the predictability that organisations once thrived on has disappeared. There are known unknowns and unknown unknowns in this unpredictable and volatile world and organisations need to create strategies that deal with that volatility. In this chapter, we will discuss our first principle of the Future Business Formula – strategy – including the techniques that organisations can embed in their businesses to begin to deal with this new world.

In the 1960s, strategy was about competition and, therefore, mostly about price. In the late 1970s and 1980s, according to Ovans' article 'What is strategy, again?', Michael Porter informed business owners that there was more to competition than price.[7] He believed that strategy came down to two options:

1. Do what everyone else is doing, but spend less money doing it.

2. Do something that no one else can do.

The first option required organisations to drive efficiencies and compete on price, causing profitability to decline for the whole industry. Often, the strategy team sat isolated in an ivory tower, created the annual strategy pack, threw it over the wall for delivery and then took no further part in proceedings. Execution was assumed to be a linear, deterministic extrapolation of the strategy document. Strategy process is finetuned for this approach. Today, strategy needs to be more about option two – doing something new, building on what you already do and reacting opportunistically to emerging possibilities. It sounds obvious but our strategic frameworks are built for a previous time when the world was more linear. A new approach to strategy is required. Strategy has to happen in real time if it is to meet the pace of change in the modern world and drive the organisation from an efficiency mindset to an innovation mindset.

Adaptive strategy for an unpredictable world

In this unpredictable world, the entry barriers into any industry are at an all-time low, meaning it's no longer about keeping an eye on what your traditional competitors are doing. It is also important to be aware of non-traditional competition who can enter your market quickly, cannibalise your products and services and steal your customer base.

Strategy needs to be flexible so it can respond to the constantly changing VUCA dynamics. Your vision can be fixed, but the path you take to get there will flex and adapt depending on what emerges on the journey.

An adaptive strategy lets direction emerge as the context evolves and becomes apparent. There is constant learning, experimentation and risk-taking through an adaptive, incremental process where we don't think too far ahead since we know the future is unpredictable. Instead, we stay in the present and sense and respond to a future that emerges in front of us. Does that mean we risk not hitting the end point? Maybe – but is it better to be a heat-seeking missile that adjusts as the target moves or a cannonball that, once fired, maintains its preordained trajectory and impact point, irrespective of whether the target is mobile?

With an adaptive strategy, a new set of actions or behaviours is required. Where organisations have put agility into delivery by implementing the principles of experimentation, fast failure and continuous learning, those same principles must be applied at a strategic level too. In a battle, armies do not go from their existing territory to the final destination in one leap. They sense and respond, taking one territory at a time and facing challenges along the way. The path they choose may be different to the one they set out to take. The military approach to strategy is to look at and prepare for many possible scenarios, knowing that what happens on the ground will change and evolve rapidly. They prepare their teams for every eventuality and allow decentralised decision-making to find the best solution based on the context.

Looking at adaptive strategy exemplars, Amazon is a great case study. You get the sense that you are watching a chess game unfold, in which Amazon is thinking multiple moves ahead along several fronts. Its opponents seem to struggle and fail while Amazon continues to systematically dismantle them. Amazon started with an online bookstore but is now the number one cloud technology provider in the world, with AWS accounting for 13% of Amazon's revenue, but generating nearly three-quarters of their operating profit in 2021.[8] A capability it created to optimise its business model unexpectedly created an opportunity to sell this expertise to customers, enabling it to diversify and grow. AWS now provides Formula 1 with a range of customer services including real-time analytics for the global broadcast audience.[9]

Some organisations have been less successful despite huge investment. Telefónica, the multinational tele-communications business headquartered in Madrid, created its Telefónica Digital brand in 2011. This was a bold experiment to greenhouse key digital projects to better accelerate the company's transformation through a new business model. Despite doing a great job of creating a new non-telco business model, the unit was shut down in 2014 as the model reportedly failed to achieve its monetisation targets.

This is less about predicting upfront the path you'll take to reach your outcome and more about sensing, responding and letting that strategy emerge over time. The journey needs to be flexible. Understand the direction you want to go in and make sure you have the strategy and the capability to roll with the punches along that route.

It's important to be able to accept uncertainty and then manage the risks effectively. Adaptive strategy requires an organisation to be comfortable with learning and testing what works in practice. Leaders do not have all of the answers – none of us is infallible – and they require humility. They must be comfortable with getting things wrong and believe that, by following an emergent path underpinned by data and insight, they will adapt and reach their destination eventually. In the Formula 1 example earlier, data and new insights clashed with experience and intuition. The result was an almost unthinkable strategy, yet it was a race-winner.

Strategy to execution

There is a disconnect between strategy and execution in many organisations, which results in a misalignment between projects and strategic imperatives. We once worked in an organisation where the strategy team admitted they had no interest in or accountability for the delivery of the strategy. Often, it is hard to know what organisations are working on. No one has seen the whole portfolio in its entirety. Even employees do not know why they are working on some projects. It is vital to ask why you are doing this and what is the strategic importance of each project in your organisation.

You have to be clear on the measures for success and how far you can nudge the dials. When you do this, how does it translate into true value? Once you know, you can assess what changes are needed to deliver that value, meet those key performance indicators (KPIs) and hit the strategic drivers. Then you can decide on the enablers required – people, process, policy, data and technology – and aggregate them into a set of initiatives. There should be a golden thread that visualises the strategic drivers, the KPIs, the business initiatives that we will undertake and the enablers required. Everything that you do will feel purposeful because there is a line of sight between what is driving the work, how you measure success and the actual work itself.

Real-time strategy and the power of data

The power of data is a key component of a real-time adaptive strategy. We need to be careful though. If you design products and services based only on data, you are potentially designing for things that happened in the past. Data should inform insights to make it actionable. If you are only watching what people have done previously, you will create a product that becomes redundant almost the moment you deliver it. The best innovators create new markets and their own white space. Steve Jobs, Elon Musk and Jeff Bezos took data and turned it into actionable insights which allowed them to innovate and create new markets. Tesla re-imagined the car and created a new market without any initial demand. The way that you buy a Tesla is different to the way that you buy any other car. The in-life experience is fundamentally different too. Engine upgrades are delivered overnight via a software update to the car in the Tesla app. Purchase an upgrade and your car will receive it on your driveway while you sleep.

We passionately advocate not prescribing change to teams, and rather giving them context about the KPIs that matter most. This means getting into a rhythm of setting clear targets every ninety days. We will refer to the power of breaking complex change down into delivering value every ninety days in Chapter 8 but, briefly, the delivery team gets into a pattern of assessing how they are performing against those targets and makes necessary changes in pursuit of those goals. It's about sensing and responding. How did the change we made yesterday affect our performance today? What did we learn from that? What will we do next? How can we nudge the dials one step further?

By taking this real-time approach, you get out of the habit of predetermining change and the path you will take and instead start to break change down to its smallest component so that you can find ways to take a step forward every single day.

Strategies to survive and thrive (COVID-19)

In the 2008 financial crisis, the liquidity problem meant that the best strategy was to hibernate and survive. The 2020 COVID-19 pandemic was different. Liquidity was not the issue. In the early stages, organisations had the choice to hibernate or innovate and, with so much uncertainty around how long the pandemic would last or how serious it would be, most decided to minimise risk. Our advice to clients was that once organisations had stabilised, they needed to innovate their way out of the situation, not hunker down and ride out the storm like last time. The pandemic forced customers to change their behaviours and needs overnight. Organisations pivoted quickly to new ways of working once they realised that people could be productive at home. Some were traditional businesses that had gone through an existential crisis and used the pandemic as a catalyst to do something different. Those that chose to stand still and hibernate started to see the competition accelerate past them. The long roll call of businesses that failed or were severely wrong-footed by the pandemic is evidence of the rigidity of traditional strategies.

Organisations that were brave enough to do something different demonstrated the right attitudes, leadership and bravery. They made changes happen in a week that would usually have taken a year. They flattened the hierarchical layers thus empowering their workforce, which in turn raised questions about the value of their middle management. In normal times, a lot of middle management drives presenteeism – employees have to be in the office where they can be seen and 'managed'. The middle manager allocates the work and manages the information flows. The pandemic meant that senior leaders had to get much closer to the teams doing the work, closing the gap between leadership and execution.

The organisations that were relatively stable during this period, as not much changed for them (for example, credit card companies), did not have the burning platform to do anything different. There was no internal imperative to revisit their traditional five-year strategy. Some of our clients at these companies recall being 'jealous' of others that were heavily impacted and shifted into crisis management as they finally had a mandate for change. Some of the stable organisations went backwards in real terms because other businesses around them were innovating; the baseline shifted.

The pandemic moved many organisations into crisis mode. Plans were thrown out of the window. We can be productive in a crisis. There is a risk that, as the new normal stabilises, we stop the behaviours and approaches that were so effective and resort to 'normal' management. We've seen this on a smaller scale when teams have production issues. A ship's bell is rung in the office and immediately the team swarms on the problem. Communication and collaboration levels increase. Hierarchies disintegrate. Team barriers come down. A single-minded focus creates highly effective working. Other team members get the coffees and the pizza to allow the key people to fix the issue. They enjoyed working like this and could achieve 'the impossible'. We asked them what happens after the issue is fixed: 'We go back to our normal way of working,' they said. Verbalising it made them pensive. Why do we go back to traditional ways of working when we know we can be better another way?

Every traditional strategy was blindsided by the pandemic. The winners were the organisations that shifted quickly to being highly adaptive, pivoted and innovated. As the pandemic recedes, do we go back to our traditional strategic frameworks and approaches or do we learn from this episode and build that winning adaptiveness into organisational capability?

Summary

Our Formula 1 story of McLaren's race strategy highlights the importance of data, cognitive diversity and left-field thinking. Traditional thinking, experience and intuition would never have come up with the idea to pit the cars in the first few laps to win the race.

Deep insight was created, a maverick idea was proposed and the team adapted to the context to create a winning formula.

Organisations need to adjust to this changing world if they are to survive. That requires new ways of working. In this chapter, we have discussed our principle of adaptive strategy, the real-time emergent strategy approach that enables organisations to sense, move flexibly and quickly reach their desired outcomes, particularly during critical times such as the COVID-19 pandemic. We have identified the misalignment between project execution and strategy and looked at how to overcome this by shortening the time to deliver evidenced value. Implementing these processes will result in an organisation that moves rapidly and stays ahead of its competition.

Actions to take

1. Study complexity and uncertainty and embrace them rather than trying to look for ways to simplify the problems in front of you. Complexity requires a different type of decision-making and approach to solving it. Build this into your strategic planning process.

2. Shift your strategic process from a traditional, linear construct to one that is emergent and adaptive, allowing your company to sense and respond to the environment around it.

3. Create a clear line of sight between your strategic drivers and KPIs through to the initiatives and enablers for change.

4. Learn from being in crisis management mode. No one wants to be in a permanent crisis but the behaviours and approaches worked and allowed you to adapt quickly. Don't lose the key factors that made you able to sense and respond quickly. Build those into your new ways of working around strategic planning.

2
Principle 2 – Customer: Create Experiences – The New Differentiator

Pit Stop – Formula 1 customers

Formula 1's response to the global COVID-19 pandemic included pivoting racing online, using F1 Esports to engage with audiences and increase engagement with Generation Z in particular. According to Formula 1, the dramatic growth in audiences saw 21.8 million views of the Virtual Grand Prix races on digital platforms alone.[10]

Using the live streaming application Twitch, four of Formula 1's younger drivers reached 2.7 million fans directly, engaging with them in real time to deliver an immersive experience in which the customers felt a genuine connection with their heroes. This was not arms-length engagement. Inviting athletes from other sports, including footballers Thibaut Courtois and Sergio Agüero, to participate in Formula 1's virtual tournament helped drive a 1,000% month-on-month growth for Formula 1's 2019 online video game, while its output across social media platforms recorded 695 million impressions.[11]

Formula 1's future plans include offering live in-game music concerts, team visits and driver interactions to fans, creating a rich environment in which the customer becomes part of the activity – an active participant rather than a passive observer.

This is not Formula 1's only customer transformation experience. As business models have broken, changed and developed, the key lessons have become

the importance of listening to your customer, stepping back to consider your core competencies and how you can drive value in a way that reflects their needs and wants.

When Formula 1 started in 1999, it offered its events to governments around the world. The result? Governments have become event customers.

In the wake of the ban on tobacco advertising, sponsorship teams offered their engineering skills and expertise to adjacent sectors – healthcare, automotive, defence, aerospace and renewable energy. Industrial organisations have become technology customers.

With the dramatic changes in the media landscape, terrestrial broadcast agreements have been replaced by a much more complex array of live and delayed terrestrial, satellite, cable and streaming. Multiplatform digital broadcast media are customers.

Yet 3,500,000 fans attend the twenty or more Grand Prix each year, buying event tickets, booking flights, hotels, hire cars and restaurants and buying merchandise. Fans are customers.

Formula 1's lesson is that today's connected environment offers a rich opportunity to engage directly with customers and that the focus has to shift from 'what we offer' to 'what the customer wants'. The two-way customer conversation has never been more important.

Customer centricity

Customers are ever-changing. The gaps between generations are bigger than ever before and customers' expectations have increased significantly. The benchmarks are no longer you and your closest competitors. Customers are now benchmarking their user experience with your company against the best digital experiences in the world, the services they use every day. Now, more than ever, customer centricity needs to be front and centre for your business.

In this chapter, we will discuss Principle 2 – the customer – and the problems of generational change, how those influence expectations, closeness to the customer and why that's important and we will give you examples of how to bring that to the fore.

Generation change

New and emerging generations want something radically different to the demographics that have been leading and running many of our organisations. Formula 1 saw its traditional customers ageing as a generation while it struggled to engage a new generation who didn't want to spend a whole day travelling to and watching a Grand Prix. While many CEOs are in the senior stages of their careers, much of the buying power and consumer influence is coming from people aged between eighteen and thirty. How these customers act, what they find important and the way they like to consume products and services are completely different to those running many of our organisations. It's easy to lose sight of what matters and what can make a difference.

Some organisations discuss Generation Z as though they are the focus of tomorrow rather than today but Dominic-Madori Davis stated that, by the end of 2020, they were responsible for almost 40% of consumer spending worldwide.[12] Their expectations for products and services are different to what we offer today, as are the ways they interact with and use technology. How many traditional organisations are listening to what they want and need?

Born in 1996 or later, they are a generation who have no memory of a time when mobile technology was not part of daily life. The early adopters in this group learned to use a touchscreen device before they could even read or write. Technology is natural to them in ways that even millennials cannot relate to.

Consumers are also moving more of their spending to experiences over products. According to a survey conducted by Harris Poll on behalf of Eventbrite, more than three-quarters of millennials surveyed indicated they would prefer to spend money on experiences with friends and family than on physical products.[13] There have been sharp increases in spending on categories like entertainment, live concerts, restaurant and travel. Driving that trend is social media. Experiences have become the social currency of a new generation of consumers who commemorate every meaningful life experience online. Experiences, not products, play out best on social media – experiences are the actual product. The product itself is almost a souvenir.

High street retailers are responding by transforming their stores into experience destinations to attract consumers away from their laptops and iPads and make a physical purchase instead. It is no longer just about the product that is stocked but about the experience that consumers have when they go into the store and their ability to capture and share that via social media channels. Restaurants are also beginning to create this 'experience' product. It is not just the meal that counts, it is how customers can document the experience on social media.

Influencers have a big impact. Stephanie Pandolph states that 85% of Instagram users follow accounts that have a style, fashion or lifestyle focus.[14] For certain segments, social media influencers have a bigger impact on people's purchasing decisions than traditional advertising and marketing.

The effect that influencer marketing can have on sports and fitness brands in particular was brought to the forefront when Nike controversially used Colin Kaepernick as the face of a new advert and saw its market value rise to an all-time high of $6 billion as a result. You can read about it in Alex Abad-Santos' 2018 article 'Nike's Colin Kaepernick ad sparked a boycott — and earned $6 billion for Nike'.[15]

Social media is being increasingly used by digital customers and, in the sixteen-to-twenty-four age group, social networks are the top product research channel. Sports and fitness brands are taking advantage of this and using influencers to show tangible results of health and fitness, as well as relatable and inspirational content.

Generation Z interacts differently. Organisations have to think about where this generation spends most of its time, and drive their services there rather than trying to encourage them into their own channels.

Consumers now demand far more immersive experiences. This is evidenced in the growth of extended reality (augmented reality, virtual reality (VR), mixed reality). In March 2014, Facebook purchased virtual reality company Oculus for $2 billion despite Oculus having only developed a prototype version of its VR headset.[16] Facebook believes that VR and Oculus have the opportunity to create the most immersive social platform ever and transform the way we work, play and communicate. The Oculus platform presents opportunities to consume content in more immersive ways. In the future, we could see a world where Facebook buys the rights to the English Premier League. If that happened, a football club could sell the best seat in its stadium with a VR camera situated on it a million times around the world for every game. Any consumer with a VR headset could get the best seat in the stadium and have a fully immersive 360-degree experience for a small amount of money. As you extrapolate the economics and apply the use case globally, it could dwarf the amount of money clubs currently receive from the Premier League TV deal.

You are not close enough to your customer

Many organisations talk about being customer-centric but most aren't. They discuss their internal customers and external customers, but they have never spoken to a consumer about what they want and need. Being customer-centric is about bringing the customer closer to the work you are doing and getting iterative feedback from them to allow you to create the right products and services quickly. It means constantly optimising the customer experience to drive high levels of satisfaction, advocacy and retention.

The fetishisation of subject matter expertise makes for unhealthy corporate cultures. It stops organisations from looking outwards and can create blind spots. We're all familiar with the product owner who is a subject matter expert, but they tend to be experts in what worked yesterday and dictate the team's path rather than talking things through.

Good product owners don't say 'you have to build in this particular way to align with this particular strategy'. They frame the commercial context, define the problem that the team must solve and set a clear, high-level goal such as 'we want a product to compete with X'.

The best product owners are servant leaders. We will discuss this type of leadership in Chapter 4. They know how to empower the team and supply what it needs. They must be good at knowing whom to speak with and what levers to pull in the organisation.

Your customer is not just your customer

No customer is just your customer. The technology helps you get the product right and the product is what brings them in and keeps them coming back. Businesses second guess and, as a result, overthink what the customer wants. They haven't actually researched what people want or how they think.

You might not be in competition with Amazon but Amazon can still put you out of business. How? People compare services. Even if you're not competing business-wise you are competing experience-wise.

Say you work for an energy company. Your customers aren't just electricity customers. They're also Amazon, Netflix and Facebook customers. People are familiar with good digital experiences and will judge you by those standards. Don't compare yourself to obvious competitors who may be similar to you; compare yourself to the best digital experiences.

Uber, the world's largest taxi company, does not own any taxis. Facebook, the world's most popular media owner, creates no content of its own. Airbnb, the world's largest accommodation provider, has no real estate. The battle now is to own the customer experience. Since the Industrial Revolution, the world has developed complex supply chains involving designers, manufacturers, distributors, importers, wholesalers and retailers. That works when billions of products are shipped and bought and moved around the world. The power of the internet, especially via mobile phone, created a movement that has destroyed those layers and moved the power.

These digital disruptors created incredibly thin layers that sit on top of those vast supply systems in which all of the costs reside, but the digital disruptors interface with people which is where the money is.

Newspapers have to write, fact-check, buy paper, print and then distribute the end product to generate their advertising revenues. Facebook simply creates a platform that is easy to integrate with and users and third parties create content which drives an audience. Facebook monetises on the back of that.

With the emergence of widespread internet access came the birth of pirate digital services. They were initially outlawed but ultimately created new markets. Napster was founded in 1999 as a file-sharing service and led the way for the emergence of peer-to-peer technology. The establishment fought to shut down Napster and other file-sharing sites to limit the damage to sales of physical media but offered no alternative to cater to the emerging demand from music fans around the world. The pirates had created a market for online music, shifting consumer behaviour so much that it allowed the likes of iTunes and Spotify to eventually develop a multi-billion-dollar industry and open up the potential disintermediation of the music business. Innovation like this is dependent on a rebel mentality, a willingness to challenge the status quo and work outside the system rather than within it.

Disintermediation – the elimination of intermediaries between producers and consumers – is a massive threat to the traditional business model as ownership of the customer relationship pivots away from incumbents. The mobile telecoms industry in the UK saw a lot of brand loyalty from customers to providers such as O2 and Vodafone in the early days, but that loyalty pivoted away from the network to the handset with the introduction of the iPhone. Consumers wanted the device and became agnostic about who provided the network access given pricing was largely the same for 'all you can eat' minutes, data and texts. If a network provider couldn't give them the device they wanted at the right price point, they moved on to another provider without hesitation. The migration process was made largely frictionless by changes in regulation which allowed for easy porting of your existing mobile number to a new network, minimising any potential disruption. Several network providers tried to counter that by developing their products and services beyond access to create some sort of stickiness, but these initiatives have largely been unsuccessful and have failed to change the dynamics.

We once had a group of C-suite executives mix with a Generation Z advisory panel. A seventeen-year-old told a banking executive, 'I'd only consider using your service if a TikTok influencer suggested it and there was a direct link from there to your bank.' The banking executive didn't even know what TikTok was.

Customer experience matters more than technology

There's rarely any conversation about what might actually deliver value for the customer. It seems obvious to differentiate between problem and remedy yet, all too often, the two are conflated: a solution is assumed rather than explored. Conventional playbooks dictate conventional solutions so technology is usually applied to solving yesterday's challenges.

Delivery teams are expected to follow a lead. That's a recipe for building stuff with potentially no value because the elements that make a real difference are missing. Pendo's *The 2019 Feature Adoption Report* determined that, based on an aggregation of anonymised product usage data, 80% of features in the average software product are rarely or never used.[17] Publicly traded cloud software companies collectively invested up to $29.5 billion in developing these features – money that could have been spent better elsewhere.

Technology then gets the blame for failing to deliver in terms of time, budget and features. These are only symptoms of a much bigger underlying issue – a failure to focus on what customers want and need.

You want to do A, B and C? Ask 'what problem do we have that A, B and C are supposed to solve?' Then the follow-ups: 'what constraints do we need to consider while thinking of a solution? What range of answers might there be to the problem?' Use all that to inform development. Principles trump playbooks. Have a consistent vision and direction but don't predetermine the path.

Technology on its own never solved anything for consumers. Ultimately, it's just logic features and functions. If you deploy those with a terrible experience over the top, customers won't adopt it. What makes the difference is a relentless focus on customer journeys and customer experience and examining data, insight and analytics to understand how journeys and experiences are performing or failing. If they are failing, what can be done differently to turn those failures into successes? Most often, the complexity of the design rather than the technology causes problems for consumers. There may be too many steps in the journey, the user experience (UX) may be too complex or the language used on the journey may be wrong. It is these nuances in the experience that need to be tweaked and adapted.

A UK telecommunications company pivoted its focus away from traditional projects to optimising customer journeys in the service space. They reorganised the team around core customer journeys and analysed each step on each journey to assess the customer's ability to successfully make their way through to completion (goal achievement). If the customer dropped out at any stage, the journey was deemed unsuccessful. A deeper analysis then took place to understand why they dropped out and the actions they took afterwards. Did they contact the call centre, for example? The transcripts of calls were added to the insights and all informed the changes that the journey teams made as a consequence.

Improving the customer experience

It's highly unlikely that most organisations could put 100% of their customer interactions into digital channels. There is always going to be a place for face-to-face or voice-to-voice support. Any interaction that is low-value, low-complexity and low-emotion works well in an unassisted digital channel. Anything that's high-value, high-complexity and high-emotion works much better with a level of assistance. You need to be excellent at both.

Many organisations have tried to go 100% digital and drive their service interactions into mobile experiences. Mobile apps work well because of the convenience and simplicity of the experience and design. When you start to include complex journeys and experiences – such as fraud issues in the banking industry, for example – they fail because they lack the level of sensitivity and emotion required to solve the problem. We are big believers in what we call an 'intentional experience'. This is a strategy whereby an organisation intentionally drives its customers to complete specific transactions in particular channels (in direct contrast to the trend for 'do anything, anywhere' omni-channel strategies) because it delivers the best possible customer experience and result.

An intentional experience drives customers where they have the best chance of getting the answer they need, right first time. High-value, high-emotion and high-complexity journeys that are driven into an unassisted digital channel are likely to fail. The customer will eventually pick up the phone, which not only increases the cost of serving their needs but also the levels of customer dissatisfaction because multiple interactions are required to complete one journey. An intentional experience requires you to balance customer insight with analytics to reveal the key interactions – the 'moments of truth' – when you should focus on meeting and exceeding customer needs. It's critical that you understand the interactions your customers value, the level of complexity and emotion, the best place to drive that interaction to ensure it's 'right first time' and that you leverage data and insight to continuously optimise the experience. You also need to drive channel migration via intentional actions (to shift high-volume, low-value transactions away from expensive contact points).

Omni-channel

Channel optimisation is about improving the operations of any individual channel within the context of its role for customers. Customers often find that channels compete with each other (eg on price) with something being cheaper online than in-store. What if customers want to use multiple channels, for example, they want to come into the store to feel a product but then order it online?

We have to consider the channel mix and the role of each channel. If something is of real value to your customer, it is up to you to design a great experience around that. This will then be the best place for the customer to go to complete their transaction to get the answer they need, right first time. You may have to add a level of personalisation and segmentation to this too. You can't create a customer strategy or intentional experience for every customer. Sometimes you need a strategy depending on the segment. Many organisations that want to differentiate will really get down to understanding what works for one customer versus another and will deeply personalise the experience.

Measure customer experience and satisfaction

There are two key messages when measuring customer experience and satisfaction. The first is goal achievement which we have discussed. Goal achievement is about measuring the success of the customer's journey and ensuring that it is driven to a point where the vast majority of people who complete the journey get the answer they need, right first time. This is a key measure which, for straightforward processes such as account management goal achievements, should be around 90%. For journeys in the digital estate that require more help and support, it should be around 80%.

The second key message is to balance goal achievement with customer satisfaction. Journeys can be designed so that people get through the process (onboarding to a service, for example) but they are not necessarily going to have a great experience. There must be a balance with a customer satisfaction measure. Many organisations use a customer satisfaction score (CSAT), net promoter score (NPS) or customer effort score (CES), which are all different things. CSAT measures the experience that the customer had. NPS measures whether the customer is an advocate – given the customer's experience, would they recommend that brand or those products and services to their friends and family? CES asks 'how easy was it to do business with us?' Often, if the customer has had a

successful journey and a great experience, they give a negative NPS. Since that measure asks whether the customer is an advocate for the brand, product or service, people often say they have had a great experience but they wouldn't recommend it for the reason they are paying too much. Based on that insight, organisations think there is a problem with the journey and invest huge amounts of money to fix it when it is not broken. What is broken is the positioning of the brand, meaning that people do not value the product or the service.

When it comes to loyalty, customers punish poor service more than they reward exceptional service. Good service helps to keep customers because people are busy and do not like to change if they are being served well. If customers experience poor service, they will

happily look for other providers. Whether it is good service or exceptional service does not make a huge difference to customer loyalty, while delivering an exceptional service is normally hugely expensive. An organisation is better off making the customer journey slick and frictionless rather than having some sections that are exceptional and other sections that are poor.

Summary

Placing the customer at the heart of what we do is critical. Customer centricity is often espoused by organisations but, in reality, it requires constant focus and effort. Few are truly good at it. In an age when all your customers are connected and every

misdemeanour is highly visible, you can't afford to be anything but passionately focused on an amazing customer experience.

Actions to take

1. The next generation of customers wants different things to your previous customers. Go to where they are. (Note: they will be increasingly nomadic between technology platforms.)

2. Benchmark and improve your customer experience against the best there is, not the

best in your industry. Your customer is not just your customer.

3. Pay more attention to the customer experience than the technology. This is where differentiation happens.

4. Define your channel mix. Omni-channel doesn't mean that every channel does everything.

3
Principle 3 – Alignment: Embrace Purpose And Transparency; Make Action Irresistible

Pit Stop – Mercedes team alignment

The Mercedes-AG Petronas Formula 1 team dominated the Formula 1 World Championship between 2014 and 2020, winning a record seven consecutive World Championships for both drivers and constructors.

Aside from a series of technically innovative cars and a team of well-led, highly qualified engineers and technicians operating out of world-class facilities, the factor which came to light in interviews given by the senior leadership, drivers and team personnel was an extraordinary degree of alignment. This was made possible by an agreed strategy and a powerful team culture which meant that everyone in the organisation understood its objectives, worked closely together across functions and departments and regularly reviewed performance and plotted improvements.

While researching his book *Black Box Thinking*, Matthew Syed spent time with the team at its headquarters and during a Grand Prix weekend, witnessing firsthand how its strategy was deployed using an open loop of communication, review and performance enhancement across the whole team. He sat in on one of the team's briefing meetings in which the drivers and key technical staff were joined remotely by the support team at the factory:

> '. . . the process was fascinating. Hamilton and Rosberg (the drivers) were taken through each dimension of performance. . . After the meeting the next optimisation loop was already underway. . .'[18]

Since only 10% of the team's staff travel to races (albeit they are supported during a race weekend by thirty to forty colleagues back at base), the entire organisation is made fully aware of the current progress in weekly or fortnightly town hall meetings.

Michael Schumacher and the Ferrari management championed the importance of this level of alignment across the organisation during their dominant period in the sport. Mercedes Formula 1's CEO Toto Wolff has taken it to the next level, ensuring that everyone who walks through the door of the business understands clear objectives, the current challenges, the degree of collaboration required to overcome them and the recognition that will be shared whenever the targets are met.

Problems begin when organisations are misaligned, whether that is misalignment of the executive team or different departments. When organisations get it right, amazing things happen. Everyone rows in the same direction and they can break through constraints. With good alignment, an organisation can overcome a structure or culture that is not ideal as long as everyone is running in the same direction. Good alignment will rally the organisation behind the cause.

In this chapter, we will discuss the third principle of the strategy pillar – alignment – and what causes misalignment. We will give you ways to bring the organisation back into alignment, increasing its effectiveness and success.

Most boards are not aligned

Misalignment can occur due to the different styles, viewpoints and approaches in a leadership team. Some leaders are strategic while others are operational and tactical. Some want to make decisions based on data and insight and others go with a gut feeling. Often, misalignment is a consequence of these preferences and the way leaders run their business units day-to-day.

Structure and discipline are important when it comes to creating alignment. If you are an entrepreneurial business that is scaling frequently, you are missing the structure and governance of large organisations, sometimes leading to misalignment. That lack of structure, purpose and mission and those varying styles, backgrounds and experiences, combined with driving people to compete rather than collaborate, can all lead to complete misalignment at a leadership layer. Silos are born at a leadership level and most executive teams do not behave like teams; they are working groups. There are three questions to work out whether that's the case or not:

- Does the team have clear objectives?

- Do they work closely together to achieve those objectives?

- Do they regularly get together and evaluate their performance?

If the answer to those three questions is 'yes', they are likely to be a team. Most executive teams we have worked with will answer no to every one of those questions. They often have individual objectives, they rarely work closely together to achieve those and they rarely review their performance and try to improve it.

No leadership team is perfectly aligned all of the time and there are varying dynamics that lead to teams getting out of sync. For example, the diverse styles

mentioned above, but also when leaders have different strategic and operational backgrounds. Of course, this diversity is important too. Cognitive diversity is key to preventing group blind spots and generating creative collective solutions, but any high-performing team needs to be multipolar. They must be able to safely suggest, challenge and debate different viewpoints to analyse problems and generate novel solutions. Once that process has concluded and the solution or agreement with the most support has emerged, they need to switch to collective alignment. This means putting aside their different views and opinions. They have all been heard but collectively have chosen a direction. It is key that they now disagree but commit. They individually may have lobbied for a different approach but now need to play as a team and accept that the group as a whole has agreed on a direction. The key is to commit 100% to trying to make that collective decision work. No half-hearted attempts, no 'I told you so', no backstage sabotage. It is difficult to put ego aside for the benefit of the team and the organisation, but it is a key indicator of a high-performing team dynamic.

Good alignment is a key differentiator in industry. We have worked with several leadership teams that have been powerfully aligned. That alignment created a compelling place to work with a melting pot of capabilities coming together behind a common goal and purpose, all believing in the values, behaviours and culture they wanted to see.

Authentic stakeholder buy-in

We mentioned earlier that an organisation's strategy can become misaligned. We have seen this happen at board level for two reasons:

1. There is a lack of incentivisation. A recent Sullivan & Stanley (S&S) client underwent a massive transformation but there was little active engagement from the senior level. We discovered that they were not incentivised to do this change work (eg through their bonus plan) and were focused on other things. We could debate the value of intrinsic versus extrinsic motivators, but we all know that incentives drive behaviour. In this case, transformation wasn't being led or supported from the top.

2. The leadership team is a passive participant.
   CEOs make decisions but no one gives their
   real views. No one has expressly agreed to the
   decision or the strategy. There is nothing worse
   than half-hearted, passive participation. Teams
   must engage in healthy debate and see different
   points of view. If the CEO decides on a direction
   you disagree with, as a member of the leadership
   team, you have a responsibility to commit 100%
   to making that decision a success.

In traditional businesses, change often needs sponsorship at the top level. With misaligned leadership teams
individually incentivised in their silos and unwilling
to enter into healthy conflict and then disagree but
commit, there is little impetus to get behind something that may not benefit their area.

Organisations need to build trust among their leadership teams. They need to spend time getting to know
each other and building rapport, relationships and
trust. They need to understand each other's motivations and respect people's different styles and
preferences. The chief executive is responsible for
ensuring that the leadership team sings from the same
hymn sheet. He or she has to listen to opinions, find
a consensus and then commit. If you do not commit
and pull in the same direction, you are going to fail.
It is important to surface those opinions in the first
place and find that common ground before commit-
ting to it and doing everything in your power to make
it a success.

Misaligned incentives in the wider organisation

Beyond leadership teams, organisations can also become misaligned through incentives. Let's say an IT department is incentivised to hit a big deadline. Their priority is getting particular expertise and capability or they risk failing. The people involved in securing that capability are usually procurement whose incentive is to save the company money. These two teams are not aligned. This results in a 'push me, pull you' effect because IT wants the best experts as fast as possible whereas procurement wants to find the lowest supplier rate they can get. This drives the use of the cheapest supplier. IT gets the C-team supplier rather than an A-team working on the project, the delivery deadlines are missed, but procurement still hits its target of an X% financial saving. The different incentives are driving competing behaviours. These 'local optimisations' are prevalent across many organisations and cause untold damage.

Local optimisations commonly occur in functionally arranged organisations. Each function tries to be the best it can be against its own targets and imperatives and ultimately becomes unconsciously selfish towards the wider organisation. The belief that, if each function can be optimised, the collective result will be optimised is wrong. We need to align each team with a higher common purpose that applies horizontally across the organisation and delivers value for customers (value stream). Then we need to optimise each function to serve that value stream (it becomes the single optimising goal). This may mean that individual functions work suboptimally in the pursuit of an optimised value stream.

Elements of alignment

There are two key elements of alignment:

- Strategy: the need to ensure a laser focus on what is necessary to drive the successful action and goals for the organisation so that a clear vision, purpose and set of strategic priorities are communicated extensively. This will remove ambiguity throughout all layers of the organisation. Without it, you find people at the coalface misaligned and working on things that have no real intrinsic value. Work then feels less meaningful and purposeful.

- Culture: in many organisations, the board only pays lip service to values and behaviours. They need to be the guardians of the culture and be committed to those beliefs. They should be role models and hold each other to account. If they are not talking about it daily at the leadership layer then it becomes insincere throughout the rest of the organisation. Boards need to think about whether they see employees as a commodity. If they do, values and behaviours are unimportant. Culture is unimportant. If you want to retain talent then values, behaviours and culture are important.

Achieving true alignment

To achieve true alignment in an organisation, people need to understand what they need to do, and why, and they need to be given the autonomy to determine how to do it. Many organisations get stuck on the 'what' and wrongly assume that everything else will fall into place. As the leader of an organisation, you have the big-picture view. It is human bias to assume that everyone else knows what we know and forget that those on the ground do not have the same context or information. As leaders, we have to translate the context around the 'why' and the 'what', so that all layers of the organisation understand what we need to achieve, and then empower employees to work out the 'how'. They will surprise you with their innovation and ingenuity. A key part of this process is over-communication. There is an old saying that people need to hear something seven times before they hear it the 'first time' and take action.

Alignment is also about prioritisation. Do not over-play intensity at the expense of clarity. You need clarity to prioritise effectively. We talk in Chapter 9 about organisational bloat where you could strip out 30–40% of an organisation and it would still function well against its core capability. We saw this during the

PRINCIPLE 3 - ALIGNMENT

COVID pandemic. Organisations suddenly developed a single purpose. They had to take their whole company remote in a matter of days, some with 150,000 people who did not even have a remote working policy. Many organisations saw productivity improve as middle management's role became superfluous.

When you have good alignment in an organisation, it is like a golden thread that runs through your business end-to-end, from strategy through to execution. Organisations often lose sight of that golden thread. It gets pulled in different directions by competing priorities, pet projects and other distractions. It is the role of the CEO and other leaders to hold onto the integrity of that golden thread, that single simple truth, that gives everybody clarity of purpose and mission and ensures that every activity links back to what you set out to achieve in the first place. Organisations make themselves so complicated and dysfunctional for no valid reason. Everybody's mission should be to simplify what they do around that golden thread. You can take out the layers, the bloat and the functions that are not adding any value and get to the heart of what matters. What matters should be clearly evident in that golden thread.

Traceability from KPIs to delivery

A business model commonly has four or five strategic priorities. Most organisations cannot focus on more. These are measured by KPIs. Once you are clear on your KPIs and how far you want to nudge the dials, you should be able to work out the impact they will have on the value you want to create. For example, if you increase online conversion, it will translate into X amount of revenue or Y amount of profit. You can then determine what changes you need to make in the organisation to create value, meet the KPIs and deliver on the strategy. Once you are clear about the changes you need to make as an organisation, you can identify the enablers required. You might find that some of those enablers already exist. If they do not, add them. Then you can determine the initiatives you need to deliver the enablers which will provide the business changes and deliver the value evidenced by your KPIs, and ultimately prove you have achieved your strategy. Full transparency from left to right and right to left.

Joining up the dots in this way allows you to assess whether investments will deliver the outcomes that matter most to you and your customers. If you can't trace it from left to right and right to left, it should not be a priority. It does not sit as part of that golden thread and you should stop doing it, freeing up valuable resources and investment.

Summary

Alignment throughout your organisation is key to effective working. This starts at the top, but it needs to be integrated throughout the organisation. Alignment does not just stop at the boardroom door. The golden thread has to run from top to bottom: from that single simple truth, which defines your vision, through to your strategy, your KPIs, how you run and change your organisation and the work that you have your people doing.

Actions to take

1. Strive for alignment at board level and accept nothing less. Difference and debate are fine but, once you have a direction, you need to disagree and commit 100% to making it a success.

2. Incentives commonly cause adverse and unwanted behaviours and misalignment between individuals, teams and departments. Prevent local optimisations by aligning incentives with a single optimising goal.

3. Push for greater transparency and a clear thread from strategy to customer-facing initiatives.

PART 2

HOW WE THINK
AND BEHAVE

The next three principles could be summarised as how we think and behave.

So much has been written about leadership and culture. A quick search on Google for each of these words (May 2022) generated 4.2 billion and 4.9 billion hits respectively. With so much knowledge about these subjects, why do we still need to talk about them? The reason is that they're so important. The image of a leader casts a long shadow and 'culture eats strategy for breakfast' (a quote attributed to Peter Drucker but with no definitive citation). Leadership and culture are closely entwined.

Leadership stories and references talk a lot about the well-known captains of industry: Steve Jobs, Jack

Welch, Marissa Meyer, Satya Nadella, etc. While they tell some fascinating visionary stories and it's great to have these demigods as icons, the truth is leadership is more of a close contact sport. You don't have to be the inventor of the iPod to be a great leader. The way we lead needs an upgrade. Leadership today is less about power, status and position. It's about creating an environment where others can flourish and creating new leaders along the way.

Culture can make or break an organisation. It is often assumed to be something that just happens – that you have little control over and is difficult to change. The reality is that there are key ways to embed the behaviours and values you want and need and other ways to stabilise and reinforce them. It's important to know the difference.

In this second part of *The Future Business Formula*, we will look at:

- Leadership
- Culture
- Talent

4
Principle 4 – Leadership: Use Your Influence For Positive Outcomes

Pit Stop – Jaguar to Red Bull

As the scale and complexity of Formula 1 have grown, along with the speed of change in a sport immersed in technology, so too have the challenges faced by its leadership teams.

In contemporary Formula 1, there is widespread recognition that only truly empowered and fearless teams work. Command-and-control leadership has given way to an enlightened and effective means of cultivating world-class teams, with each individual playing to their strengths and helping their organisation deliver world-class outcomes.

The failure of leadership styles constructed around hierarchical command and control were best illustrated when two of the automotive industry's giant companies – Ford and Toyota – entered the sport during the early 2000s. Ford, through its wholly owned subsidiary Jaguar, competed in Formula 1 between 2000 and 2004 – and never won a race during that time. Constant changes of leadership, together with a vertical reporting structure that went all the way back to its headquarters in Detroit, helped to ensure that the team of talented engineers and technicians was never able to unlock the winning code. The team was never empowered to deliver. Dissatisfaction with the team's on-track performance meant it came to be viewed as an unnecessary cost and was sold to energy drinks company Red Bull.[19]

Five years later that same team, housed in the same factory, won the first of four consecutive World Championships. What changed? Leadership style and culture. David Coulthard, who met the Jaguar management in 2004 before signing for the team – which was rebranded Red Bull Racing in 2005 – recounts in his book, *The Winning Formula*, that:

> 'Jaguar had become bogged down with reporting and layer upon layer of process. . . When Red Bull came in, they focused less on reporting the past, more on creating the future.'[20]

Command-and-control leadership at Ford became a key reason why talent employed to run the Jaguar programme never stayed long. Gary Anderson, one of Jaguar's early CTOs, said of Ford:

> 'One of its head honchos came into one of our engineering meetings in Milton Keynes and his first words to 20 or so engineers were, "You will do it the Ford way or we will get someone else that will."'[21]

Ford wanted soldiers but Formula 1 demands both soldiers and artists who can ensure operational excellence while simultaneously driving innovation and competitive advantage.

Headhunted from McLaren in 2005, Adrian Newey is Red Bull's Chief Technical Officer. In his book, *How to Build a Car*, he explains that he was immediately struck by the leadership style inherited from Jaguar, recalling that in an early meeting he was told, 'Adrian, here at Jaguar [Note; the team was by now Red Bull!] we have our procedures and processes and a way of doing things, and we expect you to fit in with them too.'[22]

That changed, since Newey is an artist, innovator and Formula 1's most successful ever technical leader, and he believes strongly in empowering talented teams. Newey relates, 'Although F1 is a technical sport, it is, in the end, a people sport. It is all about employees and creating a working environment that plays to and enhances their strengths.'[23]

Toyota's foray into Formula 1 produced no victories in eight years despite an estimated spend in excess of $2 billion between 2002 and 2009. Leadership culture required a reporting structure that led to its head office in Tokyo, with the 'Toyota Way' – a philosophy of continuous improvement and respect for people – applied with a rigidity which demonstrably failed to work in a fast-paced, agile environment such as Formula 1.[24] Mike Gascoyne, technical director at Toyota between 2003 and 2006 (including its most competitive season), noted in his lecture for Performance Insights at the London Business School in 2016 that, 'When I was sacked, I was told that the company did not pay me to make decisions based on personal expertise.'[25]

Winner of seven consecutive World Championships for drivers and teams between 2014 and 2020, the dominant team in Formula 1 today is Mercedes-Benz led by Austrian businessman and entrepreneur Toto Wolff. His leadership style could not be more different from the command-and-control world of Ford and Toyota. This is aided by the fact that he is a shareholder in the team which is autonomous from its parent company Daimler.

Of leadership, Wolff says:

'It is all about hiring and developing the right individuals, forming a culture and a team spirit around them and defining the core objective.

Once that is defined, we leave it to each other
in our respective fields. . . we are a group of
2,000 leaders. . .'[26]

As for command and control, Wolff believes strongly
in empowerment and accountability and in creating a
dynamic environment in which staff are encouraged
to contribute their ideas, innovate and challenge their
leaders. He is an advocate of tough love in the context
of a fully aligned team that has been provided with
a framework within which everyone contributes to a
process of continuous improvement. 'I make sure they
do not say yes a lot,' is Wolff's summary of a team full
of ambitious high performers.[27]

When we talk about the future of any organisation's
business, our anchor point must be leadership. In this
chapter, we will unpack the principle of modern leadership, including the characteristics, behaviours and
capabilities required of leaders in the twenty-first century and discuss how leaders can create a supportive
environment in which people truly flourish.

The problem of leadership

Leadership has a problem. The steam engine in the
eighteenth century led to the First Industrial Revolution, allowing production to be mechanised and
driving social change as people became increasingly

urbanised. During the Second Industrial Revolution, electricity and other scientific advancements gave us mass production. The Third Industrial Revolution, beginning in the 1950s, saw the emergence of computers and digital technology. This led to the increasing automation of manufacturing and the disruption of industries including banking, energy and communications.

The Fourth Industrial Revolution, according to the World Economic Forum in 2016, is upon us.[28] Blurring the boundaries between the physical, digital and biological worlds, it entails a fusion of advances in artificial intelligence (AI), robotics, the Internet of Things (IoT), 3D printing, genetic engineering, quantum computing and other technologies.

The inconvenient truth is that, despite those huge leaps in industrial change and fundamental revolutions in how we work, leadership principles and practices have barely evolved over 100 years or more. While technology has innovated at speed, how we lead and manage hasn't. Power hierarchies, functional separation, reductionism, individual performance quotas (evaluations) and reward and punishment as motivators were great for the Industrial Revolution when there was high standardisation, low competition and the machine was the solution for value creation – but we moved on. The information/knowledge age

brought high customisation, global competition and humans as the solution for value creation. Despite this, we forgot to change how we lead and manage.

Imagine if the same stasis had happened in childcare. In the 1920s, JB Watson was the eminent authority on childcare. In his book, *Psychological Care of Infant and Child*, he gave advice such as, 'Never hug or kiss them. . . Shake hands with them in the morning. Give them a pat on the head if they have made an extraordinarily good job of a difficult task.'[29] Thankfully we have developed a greater understanding of child development and have fundamentally changed our advice and practices. Management has not made the same progress.

Leadership is a privilege, not a right

Leadership is not a right. You are in a leadership position because you are deemed to have qualities and behaviours that can have an impact on others. Many leaders forget the effect their words and actions can have, not only on how somebody feels when they are at work but also in their personal lives. As leaders, we have a responsibility to ensure that we send people home to have great evenings with their families.

As a leader, you need to think about your vision and the outcomes you want to achieve and focus on how you inspire and encourage people. Your aim is to create an environment where people flourish, not a place where people hide, scared of stepping out of the

shadows or saying something that might be contentious. Leadership is about serving, not servitude. It is not about managing and controlling. It is about treating people like grown-ups and accepting that they are genuinely trying to do good work. How you deal with the exceptions will shape the leader people see you as. Listen, understand, encourage and coach.

There is no leadership without a team. Your role as leader is to guide, shape and focus people's potential towards a specific result. Use your influence for positive outcomes. If your team feels valued by you, you will be rewarded with innovative, empowered team members.

Types of leadership

There are many types of leadership. Although we might not call ourselves by any of these names directly, we will recognise ourselves and others in their behaviours. Research has looked at how effective certain styles are.

Rarely effective leadership styles are:

- **Autocratic**: these leaders make decisions without input from people reporting to them. Employees are neither considered nor consulted prior to decisions and are expected to comply. In the Pit Stop at the start of the chapter, we heard how

Ford's leaders led their failed Formula 1 team with an autocratic style.

- **Bureaucratic**: these leaders stifle anything that doesn't conform with established processes and policies (and beliefs).

Sometimes effective leadership styles are:

- **Transactional**: these leaders motivate through incentives. They reward employees for precisely the work they do. They are interested in output rather than outcomes.

- **Permissive**: these leaders are hands-off and have full trust in employees. While liberating, this style can have shortcomings around alignment and personal growth.

- **Transformational**: these leaders are always transforming, improving and pushing people outside their comfort zone. This style can become more about company growth and less focused on the individual.

Commonly effective leadership styles are:

- **Democratic**: these leaders listen to employee inputs before making decisions.

- **Strategic**: these leaders are able to bridge the strategy to execution gap and align people with the bigger picture.

- **Coaching**: these leaders focus on employees' individual strengths and make the team work better together.

We are rarely one type of leader alone. You may notice yourself in a few of the above descriptions. Autocratic, bureaucratic and transactional are the leadership styles of the industrial era when thinking and doing were separated, work was standardised and quotas were enforced. This is called a 'command-and-control' style and is still worryingly popular today. New leaders tend to emulate the way they were led and so this style is perpetuated.

The command-and-control leader:

- Assumes leadership is about hierarchy, position and power
- Controls what happens
- Allocates the work
- Controls knowledge
- Holds the power

Democratic, strategic and coaching leaders focus on alignment and autonomy. By helping to bring the bigger picture to life, focusing on employee strengths and awareness and using empowerment, they decentralise decision-making to the people closest to the work. First proposed by Robert K Greenleaf in 1970, this is called a 'servant leadership' style.[30] Some may be put off by the term servant and we could use different terms but essentially the leader serves their team to enable them to be the best they can be.

The servant leader:

- Assumes leadership is about serving people

- Owns the why and what and delegates the how

- Empowers teams

- Trusts and supports employees

- Fosters accountability

- Encourages innovation

With command-and-control leadership comes disempowerment which results in compliance and a mentality of 'stay in your lane'. A servant leader nurtures employees by empowering, trusting and supporting them and allowing them to experiment and innovate.

Over the last 100 years, it was the people's job to serve the leader rather than the leader's job to serve people. The traditional command-and-control structure is a hierarchical pyramid in which the leader is at the top and the organisation sits underneath. Servant leadership metaphorically turns this pyramid upside down so that the organisation and the employees sit at the top and the leader sits below them. This requires humility and a focus on people rather than yourself.

Rather than focusing on being the most important person in the room and telling employees what to do, the leader's mantra should be 'how can I enable people to do their best work?' This requires a completely different mindset and an acceptance that one individual does not have all the answers. This is about the power of many and how to get the best out of people.

Every organisation has two distinct groups of people – those that run your business and those that innovate. In *Loonshots*, Safi Bahcall describes how inventing new products or strategies to stay ahead of competitors is important.[31] Unless you can consistently deliver those products to customers on time, on budget and to specification, you will eventually be beaten by your competition. Leaders need to balance radical innovation with operational excellence.

Safi Bahcall describes innovators as artists and those that run your business day-to-day as soldiers. A regimented, predictable environment at the core of your business gets the best out of soldiers. Artists thrive on creativity and the freedom to express what they can do. A balance must be struck as your organisation needs both. You might create a dynamic that gets the best out of artists but end up marginalising your soldiers, impacting your ability to run the business effectively day-to-day. Equally, if you create an environment that only gets the best out of soldiers, you'll lose your artists or struggle to attract them. The art of the twenty-first-century leader is to create an environment that gets the best out of soldiers and artists, bridging the divide between and respecting the value both groups bring to the organisation every day.

Key attributes of the twenty-first-century leader

Empathy

The most essential attribute of a twenty-first-century leader is empathy. This is critical to lead your team effectively. It is impossible to provide context without emotional intelligence and, without that, you

will struggle to empathise. You have to be aware of how you are perceived. Leadership is not about one person. It is not about you. Leadership is only apparent in the context of others. Focus less on being the most important person in the room and more on how you can create experts and new leaders at all layers of the organisation. Talent will emerge from the most unexpected places.

Empowering

When you start to remove the layers of hierarchy and the boundaries that force people to conform, the organisation becomes about capabilities and encouraging people to share their points of view irrespective of status and experience. That is why it is so important that modern leaders genuinely empower people, ensuring that the right support structures are in place and that they do not undermine people by being dismissive, controlling and interfering.

Tough love

There will be times when you need to be tough, but that does not mean you have to resort to command and control. When the principles agreed as a business are not met, you need to seek to understand why and nudge employees in the right direction. Dialogue and conversation with those who are not performing are far more effective than dictating to them what to do. Instead, listen, understand and coach.

Coaching

Coaching has been shown to vastly improve people's performance and engagement and yet, in many organisations, coaching is not seen as important. A coach asks powerful open questions to raise your level of situational and self-awareness to help you come up with new solutions. We have seen amazing turnarounds from people coached on their performance. There is one caveat. If someone does not want to change, do not waste your time on coaching. No amount of coaching will make any difference. They must want to change and develop.

Autonomy and alignment

Twenty-first-century leadership is about the balance between autonomy and alignment. A leader's role is to help the team understand the 'why' and the 'what', but then let them work out the 'how'. Once the team has context and alignment and is able to act autonomously, innovation and empowerment often appear.

Culture vulture

Individual leaders influence culture every day, often subconsciously. That influence becoming a company culture requires an alignment of beliefs, values and behaviours among your peers. Often, they are misaligned, creating many tribal micro-cultures. You need to be a role model as a leader. This means being mindful of what you are doing and reflecting on how that affects the culture of the organisation.

Systems thinker

The leader also needs to enhance the system by improving policies, procedures, people and interactions. To do that, you must embrace complexity. A systems-thinking mentality is essential to work out how to optimise the system in front of you. When we work with clients, we help them study the system and they discover (often dysfunctional) things about it that they never knew. During systems-thinking exercises, they often realise they can tackle things differently.

Change agent

Change needs to be constant, moving from being an activity (sporadic, turbulent, when needed) to a capability (continual, normalised, inherent). As the leader, you set the expectation that we're going to experiment, learn and improve. You then support teams in that process and make it a safe place to learn. Change creates a chasm, a void, and there are two possible responses. The first is to put your faith in learning and the direction in which you are going, and step forwards into the chasm. That takes courage and support from above. The alternative is to step back from the void, to seek safety in the stability and structure of the status quo. Many step back. Helping your people to step forward into new change is key. They will need context, support, encouragement and trust from you as a leader.

New leaders

Leaders create new leaders. There's an old saying that if you get lucky enough to get to the top floor, it is your responsibility to send the elevator back down again. You need to think about how to replace yourself and create a breeding ground for the business leaders of the future by providing opportunities for others. True leaders don't create followers, they create new leaders.

Leading Generation Z

We are on the cusp of the next generation of consumers and employees. The twenty-first-century leader needs to understand this to attract the next generation of talent and customer. In 2020, Generation Z influenced 40% of consumer spending around the world and that percentage will grow year by year. Generation Z's expectations of products and services and their relationship with the workplace are different to other generations. From a career perspective, there will need to be a mutual value exchange between them and their employer. Otherwise, they will opt out and go elsewhere. A transactional relationship in which you hire employees to carry out tasks and give them limited value in return will be challenging to maintain;

value needs to move beyond a salary and benefits. It is akin to a 'transformational tour of duty' where the employee learns and grows and their contribution to their organisation delivers tangible outcomes. Their engagement will only last as long as that tour of duty offers mutual value. Twenty-first-century leaders need to create an organisation that attracts and retains this talent by moving away from transactional work that sees people as cogs in the machine and focuses instead on solving complex challenges that drive outcomes rather than outputs, ensuring people feel valued rather than anonymous or expendable.

It's apparent that many organisations do not understand the impact of Generation Z. They continue to design their organisations, products and services for a declining demographic and may soon find that they no longer have a business designed for growth. How many businesses are brave enough to appoint Generation Z representatives to their advisory boards to talk to executives about what they want from their careers and about their expectations for future products and services? Their insights and guidance will be invaluable.

The game-changing nature of businesses engaging with Generation Z became clear to Formula 1 during the course of the global COVID-19 pandemic. Faced with the cancellation of live events, Formula 1 used its three-year-old Esports division to create a series of online championships and one-off events. The result was 30 million Generation Z, Generation Alpha and millennial viewers watching professional Formula 1 drivers competing online against professional computer gamers and pro-celebrity guests. In 2020, 237,000 computer gamers tried to qualify for online public competitions organised by Formula 1 demonstrating that, for these younger audiences, the connected world represents an opportunity to participate rather to merely play the role of passive consumer.[32]

As a result of Formula 1's experience during the global pandemic, Esports is set to become a central pillar of this sport's strategy, its contribution to the business accelerated by an estimated five years thanks to Generation Z's readiness to embrace online, connected content.

Summary

Leadership is a privilege. Our actions and words have a fundamental impact on people and their lives. In an age of disruption, what are the attributes needed for great leadership that creates an environment where people flourish and the focus is on leaders serving rather than demanding servitude?

The Pit Stop case study of the losing Jaguar team transforming into the World Championship-winning Red Bull team is a great example of the effect of leadership. Most of the team remained the same, but new leadership, complete with an inspiring vision, created the environment and culture that turned the team around.

Empathy is critical. Emotional intelligence facilitates our capacity for resilience, motivation, reasoning, stress management and communication and our ability to read and navigate a range of social situations and conflicts.

Leadership is about the power of many. Focus less on being the most important person in the room and more on how you can create experts and leaders, even in the most unexpected places. Concentrate on motivating a diverse workforce. The changing demographics and expectations of today's emerging talent require lifelong learning, tours of duty and more meaning at work. Empower people to find solutions to complex

challenges. Ensure support structures are in place to help them succeed.

Treat people like grown-ups. Do not undermine by controlling or interfering: guide, coach, help and listen. Create a meritocracy that goes beyond performance and rewards behaviours, shifting the dynamic from colleagues as competitors to colleagues as collaborators.

Actions to take

1. We must unlearn the leadership assumptions of the past and relearn and practise a more progressive style (servant, intent-based and democratic). Command and control are no longer an option. Business is a people sport. Turn the pyramid upside down.

2. Start experimenting with new approaches to leadership. You won't be perfect and don't need to be, but you do need to try to improve every day.

3. Leading Generation Z will be different to leading millennials and Generation X. As a leader, you need to adapt.

4. Stop micro-managing. Let go of the reins and start leading from the back of the room.

5. Create a Generation Z shadow board to illuminate generational blind spots you may have in your current board.

5
Principle 5 – Culture: Be Intentional About Creating A Positive Culture

Pit Stop – culture change

As we saw in the last chapter, the leadership recruited to transform Jaguar's Formula 1 team into Red Bull Racing encountered a group of people used to command-and-control leadership, with some senior staff adhering rigidly to existing ways of doing things. Underperformance was built into the system.

It became clear to technical director Adrian Newey that some leaders within the business were not aligned, forming tribes which stood in the way of creating a unified team with a common purpose. Certain that people were pulling in different directions, Newey brought in an HR consultant who helped to identify three individuals who were saying one thing but doing another. All three were sacked. 'The change in atmosphere almost overnight was remarkable,' recalls Newey, 'The other quasi-militants over whom I had a question mark turned around, possibly relieved to be free of a mistaken loyalty to their outgoing bosses.'[33]

Newey also took steps to improve communication and increase interaction between engineering teams, physically relocating departments to a single building. He began to drive a culture shift in which meetings could '. . . only be deemed a success if a clear set of ideas and actions came from them.'[34]

The culture shift within Red Bull Racing was established early on, thanks to a keynote address by Dietrich Mateschitz, owner of Red Bull. Visiting the workforce in November 2004, he described his passion for the industry along with his vision: to win the Formula 1 World Championship within five years. This would become the company's purpose. Key to his approach was a determination to give the workforce the support and opportunity they needed to achieve this ambitious goal.

Five years later, Red Bull Racing finished second in both the drivers' and constructors' World Championship and then went on to dominate both for four consecutive seasons between 2010 and 2013. A change in leadership and culture and a team alignment around a common purpose transformed a group of people in the same factory into the dominant force in their industry. Innovative and disruptive, it was a collective effort born out of every individual being given the opportunity to excel.

Mercedes-Benz Formula 1 took and accelerated the same approach, dominating the sport between 2014 and 2020. That organisation's leadership understands the power that comes with creating a best-in-class culture. James Allison, Chief Technical Officer of the Mercedes-Benz team, believes that, in something competitive, (cultural) differences create the edge that enables one team to prosper over another. 'What we have enjoyed in Mercedes is that everybody stands up for their teammates in a way that feels very supportive and open,' he adds.[35]

Allison's view is that pointing the finger at people and saying they are to blame is forbidden. At Mercedes Formula 1, the leadership team tries to also ask teammates who are low down in the hierarchy to take large amounts of responsibility. In their experience, the more brains they can get onside in their championship battle, the more powerful they are as a group.

Mercedes' approach to creating the right behaviours and team culture includes a rigorous analysis of performance and staff being held accountable for their contribution to the team's goals. The flip side of accountability is a high level of recognition both for the entire team in achieving its goals and for individual contributions. In this way, the talent within the team is constantly motivated to improve, to become the best version of themselves and to contribute towards the team's purpose.

In this chapter, we will explore the fifth principle – culture – which is a social construct of values, behaviours and interactions between people that are seen as the norm in an organisation.

It has been proven repeatedly that an engaged culture with high levels of involvement, consistency and adaptability, and a transparent mission, improve sales, performance and customer satisfaction. An example of the causality of culture and performance comes from Queen's University Centre for Business Venturing in Ontario, Canada. Using data over a ten-year period and comparing employee engagement surveys and company results, it found that organisations with an engaged culture had:[36]

- A 65% greater share price increase
- 26% less employee turnover
- 20% less absenteeism
- 15% greater employee productivity
- 30% greater customer satisfaction levels

Culture often feels difficult for managers and leaders to interact with, comprehend and influence. There is often talk of role modelling and living and breathing the culture, but what does that mean? It feels inaccessible. We will explore how you as a leader can directly influence culture. Sometimes it's considered the softer, fluffy stuff and viewed as redundant next to drive, intensity and management by the numbers. The reality is culture is everyone's responsibility but leaders play a significant role in setting the organisational scaffolding that their teams can work within, filling in the gaps as they go.

Toxic culture

Knowing that culture is critical for people and therefore company performance, it's useful to first consider what happens when it goes 'wrong'. Unfortunately, some cultures have a devastating effect on an organisation. These types of toxic cultures include:

- High competitiveness (tournament culture)
- Everyone in it for themselves
- Artificial harmony
- Need to know basis
- Lack of trust
- Passive-aggressiveness

When we describe a culture like this, we are simply stating the dominant observable behaviour. Even toxic cultures will have some redeeming qualities. Any one culture can be described in many ways, hence the complexity of this subject.

Your culture is shaped by the worst behaviours that you, as a leader, are tolerating. Values that are not fully defined or upheld can drive toxicity because they are misinterpreted or ignored. We have seen accountability as a value misinterpreted and articulated as 'one throat to choke'. Culture should translate from specific values into observable behaviours, actions, processes and how you run your business. If the way you work is not in line with your values, the processes you use day-to-day are completely misaligned.

Many organisations talk about empowerment, yet the leaders dictate, resulting in teams becoming passive. Change becomes a dirty word and things stay the same because they have always been done that way. Corporate inertia can create incredible resistance to change.

If we believe that leadership influences culture, then the things every leader does impact culture. The reality is that most leaders are not aligned with the behaviours that drive a particular set of values, assumptions and culture and small pockets of difference develop, resulting in conflict and different tribes of people working within different cultures in the same organisation. This is why culture is so difficult to articulate. Culture is far more about social understanding and accepted behaviours than about the values written on a wall.

Behaviours are important because they are cultural currency – they are where the culture can be observed. Culture, values, mindset – none of these can be seen or observed, but behaviours can.

Culture is no one thing across the organisation. It is made up of micro-cultures within specific departments. The risk and finance department will have a different culture from the sales department. This is in part driven by personalities because micro-cultures are created where there are clusters of like-minded types of people.

Inspire and empower versus command and control

The currency for economic growth in business in the twenty-first century is knowledge and ideas. Leadership that is focused on one person dictating all of the ideas and specifying the plan is no longer relevant. As we said in Principle 4 (leadership), the power of many rather than the person with the highest status is what will make the difference in the future. The leader must have the humility to accept this and invert the pyramid so that they are no longer at the top with the resources at the bottom. Think about the emerging talent coming out of universities – young people with brains and fresh ideas. In traditional organisations, they are buried at the bottom of the pyramid, stifled by hierarchy and unable to elevate their ideas and concepts. They are the next generation of consumers too. If you are trying to create products and services and deliver an organisation that is going to serve the next generation of consumer, then you need to understand those dynamics from the very people who fit that demographic within your own business. It's time to elevate them.

Leaders in twenty-first-century business need to ensure that this non-hierarchical, non-authoritarian attitude exists in their culture. That doesn't mean an abdication of responsibility and full-blown democracy, but rather an environment that gets the best out of people. Leaders need to understand what motivates different demographics within their organisation. They have to accept that what worked for the long-term traditional employee of the past will not work for the type of employee they are going to have to manage over the next ten to fifteen years.

In Edgar Schein's work, *Organizational Culture and Leadership*, he describes six primary embedding mechanisms that are the major tools for leaders in helping organisations think, feel and behave.[37] These visible artefacts of the culture give us insights into how to role model them.

The primary embedding mechanisms are:

1. What leaders regularly pay attention to, measure and control

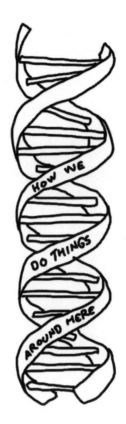

2. How leaders react to critical incidents and organisational crises

3. How leaders allocate resources

4. Deliberate role modelling, teaching and coaching

5. How leaders allocate rewards and status

6. How leaders recruit, select, promote and excommunicate

He also describes six secondary reinforcement and stabilising mechanisms:

1. Organisational design and structure

2. Organisational systems and procedures

3. Rites and rituals of the organisation

4. Design of physical space, facades and buildings

5. Stories about important events and people

6. Formal statements of organisational philosophy, creeds and charters

The twelve items are listed in order of most to least powerful, with the most powerful at the top. In reality, they must be used together. We often see the bottom six used to try and shift culture but rarely the top six. Often organisations start with the twelfth – some new values and statements of harmony. They may change the physical space, ways of working or structure or create an internal PR campaign but these are only useful for stabilising and not embedding culture. The top six are what leaders need to align on and role model. The pandemic exposed the second – most of us witnessed the true values of organisations during that time, for example, airlines whose rhetoric potentially compromised customer safety to keep revenue flowing. The sixth mechanism is a great lens on which types of behaviours are tolerated and which are revered. We find this model useful towards helping to create a multifaceted approach to culture change and answering the common question about how leaders influence it.

Trust, respect, honesty and transparency

The first three of these values – trust, respect and honesty – are prerequisites for any modern organisation. If you don't have these then you may as well give up now. The fourth, transparency, makes your culture different. Too many organisations still have a parent-child mentality of sugar-coating messages. They do not talk openly and honestly about challenges they are facing or fear of failure or demonstrate weakness out of concern that it could count against them. They have performance management processes that encourage competition rather than collaboration with peers. When transparency is lacking in an organisation, employees don't feel trusted; exposing a weakness sometimes has negative consequences. Transparency is the smart cut to trust, respect and honesty.

A culture of openness and transparency can feel uncomfortable at times. A new level of trust is required and there is no place to hide, but it is revered by those who experience it. Transparency will expose your dysfunction and shortcomings, but you need this to be able to fix them.

Attributes of high-performing teams

Sometimes, culture at an organisational level is too big to influence significantly. We are advocates of starting small with change and allowing positive peer pressure and social copying to help spread and scale it organically. One way of doing this is to focus on nurturing a great culture in discrete, high-performing teams. The team members have a common sense of purpose which is completely aligned with their mission statement. They know what success looks like and the measures needed to achieve it. They are empowered to use their expertise to work out the best way to achieve those goals. We call this the 'speed-to-value' accelerator.

In one organisation, we had to drive a high level of performance in a quick period. We gave one team the target of achieving three outcomes within ninety days but without dictating how they should do this. They were given support to be successful, for example, access to data and the ability to make changes daily. Leadership was adapted from the classic direct, monitor-and-report role to one that provided support and protection and removed blocks. Traditional processes were bypassed. The team could challenge the status quo and flourish. The technical people challenged the commercial people and vice versa because they all had skin in the game. They were aligned through a common sense of purpose and, critically, their team incentives were aligned with that purpose too. As a result, they achieved the target in under forty

days. In the process, we created an energised, empowered team. It's not that difficult and we have done this for many clients. The trick is making it sustainable; hence why we also trial a different style of leadership.

We advocate using an exemplar team that demonstrates new ways of working and new cultures by operating in our S&S speed-to-value 'glass tube' concept. We will discuss this in more detail in Principle 8 (change and delivery) but, briefly, they are encouraged to intentionally do things in a different way that challenges the status quo while also making their actions visible to the rest of the organisation. This requires strong leadership to protect that team and the new ways of working from the inevitable rocks that will be thrown at them because this way of working is so different. The new approach leads people who are not taking part to adopt some of the exemplar team's behaviours and practices and the change starts to become viral. The grassroots movement starts to get a groundswell of support and permeates throughout the whole organisation.

Trust is essential in a high-performing team. Often, people think that trust takes time and needs to be earned. We think trust simply takes courage. Instead of waiting for someone to prove they are trustworthy (an ironically untrusting approach), give them the benefit of the doubt and have the courage to trust them implicitly. Few people are untrustworthy. You may have to deal with untrustworthiness occasionally, but that's leadership for you. Many reward you with complete trustworthiness when you give them space to spread their wings. Others need a gentle nudge and some coaching to get there in the end. The point is that trust comes from trust. We have seen deep trust develop in days when one person had the courage to step into the middle first. With trust, the team can start to challenge each other around the purpose because, as a group, they want to achieve the right outcome. They will confront the difficult issues, have healthy conflicts and find their way through them.

Since they are a peer group, members of a team tend to act as if they are all at the same level, which can sometimes drive problems in decision-making. They will first have healthy debate, hearing everyone's voice and ensuring everyone feels their opinion is valid. Naturally, a group like this may want to have consensus but, in our experience, this rarely happens, especially if you have created a diverse team to get as much knowledge in the room as possible. They then have to resort to voting or defer to a leader to make the final choice once all options are heard. The key part is what comes next. As a high-performing team, they will disagree and commit. Those who disagreed with the final decision will accept that decision and then commit 100% to playing their part in making the decision a success. This is a key attribute to the success of high-performance teams. When seen in action, it is a force of nature.

A culture of celebration

All organisations need to understand what 'good' looks like. Some organisations have a clear view of where they are and where they want to be but still reward success in the same old way using individual performance reviews. They want to move to team outcomes, but instead promote and give bonuses to individuals. They want collaborative teams, but instead reward heroes. When you celebrate community from a cultural point of view, it helps the rest of the organisation understand what is recognised and rewarded and becomes a positive reinforcement mechanism.

There is also a difference between employee recognition and employee appreciation. Employee recognition is about performance and recognising success. In most organisations, there is more failure than success, but failures can be an important asset. While it is good to recognise when somebody does a great job, it is even more important to appreciate the value of somebody when they fail. Notice how the language is different. Recognition says 'You've done a good job. This is great for the organisation', but appreciation says, 'You are a valuable member of our team,' and you recognise the value a person brings to the organisation, irrespective of whether they have succeeded or failed.

Culture is a set of observable behaviours

Often, an organisation's statement about its culture is different to reality. It becomes merely an aspirational guide because it does not break down into observable behaviours, which are the currency of culture.

Culture and behaviours do not travel by PowerPoint, but so many people think they do. Many organisations have a set of corporate values that do not mean much and are espoused rather than real. Enron, a company whose leaders were jailed and bankrupted because of fraud, proudly displayed the values 'integrity, communication, respect and excellence' in its lobby. Its true culture was not what they had on the wall. Often values are too high-level and can be interpreted differently by employees, from the micro-manager to the most empowering servant leader. Values have to be broken down to a level of observable behaviours so that people can see and hear examples in practice. Unless we agree what those are, there will be ambiguity and differences of opinion about what they mean.

Adrian's son's school had some golden rules. One was 'We care'. We've seen similar in organisations and always wondered what it meant. On its own, it's too broad, but the school went further – they included clear behaviours:

> 'When we see litter on the ground, we pick it up and put it in a bin.'

'We take our muddy boots off before we run
across the playground.'

'When we see someone who looks sad, we try
and cheer them up.'

This helps a group of five-year-olds know what is
expected of them and how to act in line with the core
value. The teachers were excellent at reinforcing and
recognising the correct behaviours, and redirecting
the kids when they were negligent. Even five-year-
olds were able to self-regulate and hold each other
to account:

'You don't care – you ran across the
playground in your muddy boots.'

These golden rules with observable behaviours were
coached into the children. Six years later, his son was
playing rugby when a piece of litter blew across the
pitch in front of him. Instinctively, he stepped out of his
way to trap the litter and put it in his pocket before carrying on. His observable behaviour was plain to see.

We were once coaching a client at an organisation
where the corporate lobby included a similar 'We care'
value. The client had been discussing his own core
values and one morning asked for a quick session. He
was flustered. On his journey to work, he drove past a
car at the side of the road. It was raining heavily and,
as he passed the car, he saw a woman holding a coat

above her head and looking down at a flat tyre. He could have stopped to help, but he didn't. He was late for a meeting and it was raining. As he walked past the 'We care' corporate statement in the lobby, he suddenly had a reflective moment when he realised that if he had cared, he would have stopped and helped. His boss would have been OK if he was fifteen minutes late and soaked through if he had explained why. The coaching session progressed to reassessing what values meant for him not just at work but as a human being and a good citizen.

Many organisations struggle with this concept. They do not break down the big value word into observable behaviours. If you can specify what those behaviours look like then there is no ambiguity about what is expected.

There can be too much forgiveness of bad behaviour in organisations. Things are done in the workplace that would never be accepted in any other social norm, yet they are tolerated and accepted in toxic cultures. A common theme throughout this book is about the next generation and their expectations of the workplace. They are motivated by completely different things from generations before. Work is not necessarily a transaction or about financial reward. They are looking for more and if organisations continue to tolerate those sorts of behaviours they will never attract and retain the talent they need to survive.

Cultures with purpose

Over the past twenty years, organisations have focused on attracting talent by being a great place to work. It has become about extrinsic motivators: who offers the best lunches or has the best table football, or whether they give unlimited holiday or great benefits. What humans strive for is purpose which is an intrinsic motivator. Everyone wants to feel they are doing something worthwhile. That's why start-ups are such inspiring places to work. They are no-frills environments, but everyone is aligned behind a common purpose and winning mentality. This is the difference between companies that call themselves a family and companies that focus on being like a winning sports

team. Families put up with dysfunctional behaviours and keep people close based on association. A sports team has a purpose and everyone performs to try to remain in the A-team. They win and lose as a team. It is the winning team mentality that gets the best out of people – trying to achieve goals and reach peak performance together rather than being concerned about whether this is a comfortable place to work. This is the case in Formula 1 companies.

Meritocratic cultures

If you think about it, your whole career is a competition. You start at the bottom of the pyramid and have to work your way to the top. People are commonly rewarded for tenure rather than for performance or the value that they create. A sense of entitlement starts to emerge.

A meritocracy rewards people for the value they create rather than what they do. This goes beyond performance and ties into behaviours, authenticity, culture and values. If you start to reward people for this and the way they behave, then there is no longer competition among peers. You have no choice but to collaborate to achieve success together. It starts to drive the right dynamic and culture across the organisation. If the structure is flattened, employees become less obsessed with job titles and focus more on expertise and capability. Then you start to reward people for the value of their expertise and their capability. People feel valued because their contribution is acknowledged.

Culture of accountability

Accountability is often associated with whom to blame but it is about delivering on a commitment and taking responsibility for the outcome, not just performing a set of tasks.

Accountability is needed at all levels of the organisation. Your role as a leader is to set up people and teams so that they can be accountable. This means:

- Being clear about what the outcome should be. Setting clear expectations.

- Ensuring the person or team has the skills and resources to meet those expectations.

- Measurement: agreeing on milestones, targets etc and actions if they are slipping off track (eg let me know of issues early and let's brainstorm the remediation together).

- Providing objective feedback and coaching on their progress, performance and approach.

- Providing clear follow-up. If they succeed, rewarding and repeating, and maybe increasing their remit. If they fail, considering the next steps which could be moving them to a different role or helping them find a role elsewhere.

Is there a lack of accountability in your organisation? Check if you have missed any of these factors. As leaders, we have to hold up the mirror to ourselves first.

Systems to bridge the gap

Most organisations want to innovate and be creative. The reality is that in any organisation there are two groups of people – those who have been there for some time and know how to run your business and those who want to create and innovate. It is difficult to create one culture that works for both. The result is usually a culture embedded in governance, process and rigour that upsets your creative people. Or you overdo the innovation which makes those who run your operation day-to-day feel disenfranchised. The art is to focus on systems. What works for those who need to run your business day-to-day? What works for those who innovate and create? How can you create a bridge between the two so that they each understand the value of the other? Once you systemise how these two groups work, you create an environment that works for all. What we want to do is create scaffolding around the organisation which will allow them to continually improve within the system.

Summary

Culture is the secret sauce to your organisation's performance. It can be difficult to influence and nearly impossible to articulate but it is incredibly important to success. All leaders of people need to be fixated on how people think and work. Immerse yourself in amateur psychology, behaviourism and systems thinking. There is so much information now to help us understand why people appear to be predictably irrational.

What's a positive culture? The reality is every organisation will be different but you need to start talking about it openly and starting to shape it. Involve as many positive people as possible. Start to sketch out the sacred cows and the things you mustn't tolerate. Your teams will be good at this and will want to get involved. If it's their idea, they will live and breathe it. Cocreate, don't send diktats from above. Formula 1 teams have cultures of accountability, performance and collaboration. How would people describe the culture you are responsible for?

Actions to take

1. What behaviours are you tolerating that you shouldn't be? Do something about it.

2. What are you reinforcing (by paying it attention, applying resources to it etc)? Do this consciously and with culture in mind.

3. Empowerment means you lose power and others gain it. Get comfortable with this and help people take accountability.

4. Culture is a set of observable behaviours. Give real examples and celebrate the behaviours you want the organisation to be known for.

5. Be conscious of what truly embeds values and behaviours and what simply stabilises them.

6
Principle 6 – Talent: Create The Sought-After Organisation To Work In And With

Pit Stop – young talent

When the COVID-delayed 2020 Formula 1 World Championship commenced in Austria, a figure unknown outside of the team but recognised as a key contributor to the organisation's goals joined the dominant Mercedes-Benz drivers Valtteri Bottas and Lewis Hamilton on the podium. Holly Chapman is a powertrain engineer in her twenties. A graduate of Loughborough University, she did not even follow Formula 1 until her stepfather introduced her to it at the age of sixteen, at which point she began to appreciate the complexity of the sport.

The Mercedes-Benz Formula 1 team appoints a member of its workforce at random to represent the team on the podium whenever the organisation scores a victory. The decision is made minutes before the podium ceremony. Line managers can recommend individuals to receive this uniquely public and high-profile recognition. The message is clear – every member of the team contributes to its success and recognition is not given solely to the high-profile drivers or senior team executives. Recognition is driven throughout the business.

Hiring Holly straight from university, Formula 1 team's recognised that, by recruiting young, talented staff, they create teams which have the right behaviours and values from the start. To fill this pipeline of talent, Formula 1 teams run their own internship programmes and contribute to initiatives such as Formula Student (targeting undergraduates) and F1 in Schools (aimed at twelve- to sixteen-year-olds) to ensure that there is a ready pool of talent motivated to join this sector.

Pioneering an innovative form of recognition which is both visible and applied across the entire team in Formula 1, McLaren would distribute a high-visibility 'winning shirt' to all team members after every Grand Prix victory. Not only did this mean every member of the team was seen as being equally responsible for McLaren's successes, but it was also deployed within the factory operations where 90% of the staff are based. In this way, the team's successes were not merely enjoyed by the race team, but also made highly visible across the entire workforce, front line and back office.

Getting the right talent in your organisation is incredibly important. This is why talent is the sixth principle of the Future Business Formula. We believe that the age of being thankful to have a job is gone. Organisations need to work consciously to attract and importantly host talent to become a sought-after organisation to work for and work with. We include the latter part (work with) because younger generations are less likely to talk about working in or for an organisation, but rather consider themselves to be working *with* you in a relationship of mutual value exchange. When that exchange becomes unbalanced in the organisation's favour (transactional), they may choose to move on. Younger generations are much more purpose-led. Talent starts with recruitment. If you can get recruitment right, everything downstream becomes much easier.

People are your most important asset

Organisations often refer to people as assets or human resources but that dehumanises the workforce. Beyond a piece of paper that resides at Companies House, an organisation is simply a collective of people who have agreed to work together on a common objective. There may be assets, policies and processes, but the business exists only because people agree to fulfil that common purpose together. If you are not concentrating on people as the most important part of the organisation, you are missing a trick.

How companies deal with talent

Some organisations are great at identifying talent and attracting them but cannot then host or retain that talent. In the innovation space where you want to do things differently, people are often hired to innovate but then forced to conform and work within the system they were asked to change. From day one, this talent is set up to fail and it's no surprise that they leave.

The structures and processes that get the best out of the people that run your business day-to-day are not the same as for people who want to be creative. Leaders need to be aware of this. As we said earlier, people now want a different relationship in their careers. This comes back to our point about tours of duty. People do not need to move from one organisation to another. They can have tours of duty within the same organisation. It's less about job titles and role descriptions. The best way to maximise value from your talent is to develop their expertise and capabilities by giving them a broad view of your organisation and setting them problems and challenges to solve.

Most organisations today think that the only way to reward talent is to promote them, but you can get a lot more when people take on a role that does not assume a certain position or line management. It can be an incredibly empowering activity to use talent differently without relying on waiting for 'dead person's shoes'.

Recruitment debt

Leaders have to face and deal with the recruitment mistakes they made in the past. We see poor people management in organisations which sees individuals being moved around the organisation in the hope of finding something they are good at. This only results in moving a problem somewhere else. This is different to moving people because you want to explore and challenge their capability and talent and it is important not to mix up these two motivations.

The reality is that you have to let some people go and bring in new players to create and maintain an A-team. High-performance teams do not like passengers. If people are not right for the job or are struggling to find a place anymore, you have to deal with it. They might be people who have served you well in the past, who are still good at what they do and who actually could go on to another organisation and be incredibly successful, but they are not right for your context at this time. Many leaders are unwilling to have these tough conversations and so the organisation struggles with recruitment debt.

Sometimes, organisations or teams are described as 'being like a family'. We are not fans of this metaphor. Many families are dysfunctional or have dysfunctional characters. Many adverse behaviours are tolerated because of 'family' ties. We like to think of the organisation as a sports team. We have a purpose and need a winning mindset. We also expect the skills needed to change as we progress (eg as we progress from league four to league three and upwards). Each player is expected to hone their skills and collaborate with others to achieve the required collective team performance. All players should feel the healthy tension of a need for self-improvement and team improvement. Our place on the A-team should never be assumed. We need to work hard to retain that place otherwise we should be replaced by someone better. We need to be without fear as that would be counterproductive. The role of the leader must be to create the right environment and not manage the performance of individuals. We wouldn't 'manage' the performance of a seedling to encourage it to grow but we would give it the water, sunlight and nutrients it needs.

Finding hidden talent

Talent and expertise can be found in the most unexpected places but it is sometimes hard to discover in a hierarchical organisation. If somebody carries a junior job title then they are often buried in the pyramid and rarely given a platform to speak up. In one organisation we worked with, the team was told that they were not allowed to talk in meetings that the CEO or leadership team attended, yet they were far more capable of discussing the topics we needed to talk about. By addressing this dysfunction head-on and working through the awkward bit where no one could explain why this was the norm, we ended up

creating a great platform for them to showcase what they could do and allowing the organisation to see the talent that existed at junior levels of the business.

In organisations that are less hierarchical and less bureaucratic, talent can be more easily identified. Remember that our role as leaders is to serve. It is not to dictate and demand servitude or to deliver messages but to be a spokesperson on behalf of our people. Our job as leaders is to help them flourish.

Creating the right environment

As a leader, there will be things that you are good and bad at. You need to build a team of people around you that are better than you in the areas where you are weak. Added to this, you need to give them a platform to speak up. This is the power of many coming together to make the organisation a success. Recognise that you can't do that on your own.

When people feel they can speak their views, they become proactive. The most junior people feel that their opinion matters. They challenge the status quo. It is tragic to see so many organisations failing to listen to them because they are seen as a commodity or less important. Particularly in the change management and delivery spaces, they are seen simply as cogs in the wheel to carry out a specific transaction rather than experts who can add value.

As a leader, do not expect talent to perform within your ecosystem. Your role is to create an environment where that talent can flourish.

CASE STUDY: HIDDEN TALENT

We led a major transformation initiative to create a different pattern for delivery across a major bank. We wanted somebody who would be good at structure and process, but not blindly follow it, to establish a programme management office (PMO) of the future. Someone who was looking to challenge the status quo and do things differently and who was willing to stretch themselves and take on more accountability and responsibility to push their career forwards. We identified a fantastic person with those attributes who worked in the corporate PMO, hidden down within the layers of the organisation. This was a classic case of expertise in the most unexpected place. She got right under the skin of the delivery. Not only did she run the programme office, but she understood everything that was going on in every element of the programme which allowed us to focus on the big issues and obstacles that were getting in the way of our ability to succeed. Her approach radically changed how the organisation thought about the purpose of a PMO. The traditional purpose of a PMO is to 'monitor, standardise and control'. It transformed into 'maximise the flow of valuable work'. Most executives love that statement until they realise that they don't know what work is valuable. They don't measure flow and, if they did, they wouldn't know how to improve it. By applying agile and lean principles, visualisation and flow, she made the PMO the heart of the delivery team and improved how work was done rather than just reporting on the status of the car crash. Having looked around for the potential for this colleague to move forward in the bank afterwards, it became clear that the external market could offer her better opportunities. In the end, she joined S&S and is now one of the leading PMO experts in the UK earning significantly more and doing far more meaningful work than if she'd stayed on her traditional career path.

Diversity of thinking, people and backgrounds

Striving to increase workplace diversity is not just an empty slogan. It is a good business decision. In 2015, McKinsey found that companies in the top quartile for ethnic and racial diversity in management were 35% more likely to have financial returns above the industry mean.[38] Those in the top quartile for gender diversity were 15% more likely to have returns above the industry mean. Not representing society in your organisation is probably causing you pain.

Diverse teams are more likely to be objective and keep the facts in mind. They perform better at holding each other to account, encourage better scrutiny of each other's actions and make sure that teams are aware of their own biases. You want to avoid the classic group of people with the same kind of background, age, gender, mindset, experiences and race as they are likely to have blind spots. We want to move beyond that. Tackling complex issues requires more than just intelligence and skill. It requires diversity not just of demographics (gender, race, age, religion or sexual orientation) but also diversity of the mind (cognitive diversity). The aim is to increase group wisdom so that a broad range of perspectives in the team thoroughly covers the issue at hand.

Most organisations have people who have worked with them for a long time. If you are building products and services based on what you know about your business, then you are likely to miss the mark – it has to be about the customer. This comes back to capabilities and expertise. Focus on the capabilities you need in your organisation to make the business a success rather than hiring somebody who is the same as everyone else there. Understand your customer rather than thinking you know what they want. As we said in Chapter 2, customers these days are not just your customers. They are also customers of Amazon, Netflix and Facebook. They know about good digital experiences and will judge you by those standards, not by your own or your traditional competition.

This means that you need different points of view within your organisation to give the diversity of thought that allows you to deliver products and services that hit the mark. We advocate that organisations build Generation Z advisory boards to listen to what the next-generation consumer wants, rather than assuming it. A sixty-year-old chief executive is not going to be in touch with what an eighteen-year-old wants from their service experience or the channels that they will use to consume your services.

Listening to people who have less life experience than you, but are going to help influence the future success of your organisation, requires a level of humility. Matthew Syed, in his book *Rebel Ideas*, talks about the challenges that the CIA faced during 9/11.[39] The failure of the CIA to spot the warning signs of the 9/11 plot has become one of the most hotly contested issues in the history of intelligence. New CIA recruits all looked the same – white, male, Anglo-Saxon, Protestant Americans. They had a thousand people with one point of view, rather than a thousand different points of view which would have given them a much broader view of the threats and challenges the country faced. That applies to organisations too. If you hire people who are the same as the CEO, you will have lots of passive leaders with the same opinion. It is crucial to proactively bring people in with different backgrounds, ethnicities, genders, and from different industries too, who can give you completely radical points of view on how you can win and be a success.

Embrace your rebels

Many organisations are great at finding talent but poor at retaining it. The very people hired by leaders to innovate are forced to conform to and work inside the system they want to change, suffocating their ability to be creative. The structures and processes that get the best out of the people who run your business day-to-day are not the same as those that get the best out of the people you want to be creative. Thinking and acting against the current of popular opinion is critical to human advancement.

We've long advocated a punk manifesto for twenty-first-century businesses, born out of a belief that the attitudes, behaviours and mentality that kept organisations alive during a period of relative calm will no longer work. A transactional relationship with work will not drive radical change.

What are the punk principles that could make a difference?

- Create a movement – get behind a mission and challenge the status quo.

- Have a non-hierarchical, non-authoritarian attitude. Knowledge and ideas are the main sources of economic growth in the twenty-first century. Value capabilities and expertise, not job titles and status.

- Be rebellious – disrupt mainstream and conventional thinking. Bring unique perspectives to longstanding problems.

- Be non-conformist – do not allow your views to conform to prevailing ideas or practices if you disagree.

- Be radically authentic – in an age of being oversensitive and overcautious, have an 'emperor's new clothes' mindset.

In January 1983, Apple employees who were working on developing the Macintosh personal computer went on a retreat run by Steve Jobs. The product's developers were worried that the project was losing its initial spirit as the team grew larger. To reassure and motivate them, Jobs opened the retreat by saying: 'It's better to be a pirate than join the navy.'[40] If you are bright but prefer the size, structure and traditions of the navy, then join a traditional corporate. If you are bright, you think differently and you are willing to be part of a special, unified and unconventional team, then become a pirate. There is a reason why we have a 'Jolly Roger' pirate flag at the S&S offices.

Jobs used the pirate metaphor because:

- Pirates can function without bureaucracy.

- Pirates support one another in the pursuit of a goal.

- Pirates stay creative and on-task in difficult and hostile environments.

- Pirates can act independently and take measured risks.

- Pirates embrace change and challenge convention.

The democratisation of technology means the barriers to entry in many industries are at an all-time low. Leaders need to encourage meritocratic, horizontal organisations for the knowledge age by valuing capabilities and expertise, not role profiles and job titles. Leaders must coach, not dictate, and recognise that it is their responsibility to enable others to be successful, empower teams to find the right path and ensure that they all share in the reward. They need to challenge conventional thinking. The status quo is stifling your business, stifling innovation and stifling progress. Be non-conformists. Do not accept prevailing ideas or practices that are no longer relevant in the twenty-first century. These bold, brave and courageous people are lacking in business today.

Summary

To become the sought-after organisation that attracts and retains the best talent, you first need to address your recruitment debt. Deal with the problems you've created in the past. Remember that the next generation of employees and the next-generation consumer have different expectations. They demand different experiences in the workplace and they require different experiences of your organisation's services. A radical mindset shift is required. You have to think differently about the people you bring into your organisation and how you grow them. This will then permeate through everything you do as a business – how you run it, how you lead it and how you host and develop your talent.

Actions to take

1. You will have recruitment debt that is overdue. You must deal with it.

2. Mine your organisation for hidden talent. Create a platform for younger people or junior roles to have their say and show what they can do.

3. Demographic and cognitive diversity is important. Pay attention to diversity as a leader.

4. Embrace your rebels. Your organisation will need people with a punk/pirate mindset to shake off the status quo.

PART 3
HOW WE BUILD
AND IMPROVE

Change, delivery and transformation have become commoditised. Many leaders believe they can be managed by hiring people with certifications and a 'factory' of engineers. The result is mediocrity or work that is outsourced according to the lowest common denominator which is usually cost. This is a false economy when the result is that change fails. Change, delivery and transformation are unpredictable and soft skills, experience, problem-solving, collaboration and leadership skills are more important than the certificate someone holds in a particular subject. A driving licence doesn't guarantee a good driver.

Change and transformation need to be a constant, inbuilt capability, not just an exceptional, one-time, stop/start activity. The reassuring news is that the shift from an activity focus (sporadic, turbulent, when needed) to a capability focus (continual, normalised, inherent) means this new formula will be robust, adaptive and therefore long-lived.

As organisations prepare for the future, the ability to effect change and transform will be critical to success. The way we deliver has to match the new pace of the world around us. We need to innovate, test, learn and execute at supersonic speeds. Formula 1 teams excel at this.

The deterministic delivery methods of the past that relied on meticulous plans, the division of labour into specialisms and big upfront design are limiting speed and effectiveness in this new VUCA world. The trouble is they still feel logical, even as we initiate a third replan due to missed milestones.

In the third part of *The Future Business Formula*, we will cover:

- Innovation
- Change and delivery

7

Principle 7 – Innovation: Leverage Cognitive Diversity – Allow Ideas To Flourish

Pit Stop – recombinant innovation

Formula 1 teams are obsessed with finding a competitive edge over their rivals. Although the sport is heavily regulated by the Fédération Internationale de l'Automobile (FIA), the leading teams find ways to innovate and give themselves a performance advantage in relation to technology, processes and strategy.

In 2020, the all-conquering Mercedes team introduced a steering wheel that not only steered the car left or right but could also be pushed and pulled rather like the joystick in a plane. This enabled the suspension geometry to be optimised in certain corners as the car moved through its entry, mid-corner and exit phases, giving drivers Lewis Hamilton and Valtteri Bottas a small but important advantage over their rivals – particularly in qualifying.

It is perhaps unsurprising to hear that Mercedes' technical director James Allison is an aerobatics pilot in his spare time. This approach to innovating by looking for external inspiration is common in the sport. Innovation requires innovators – people who question established ways of doing things, look for new approaches and integrate solutions in a better, more efficient way than previously.

In the 1950s, British engineer John Cooper decided to place the engine behind the driver. This was ground-breaking innovation at the time, the engine having previously been placed at the front of the car when it initially took the place traditionally occupied by horses. Cooper's designs not only revolutionised performance in Formula 1 but established a mid-engine layout used by all supercars to this day.

Each subsequent decade has seen similar step-changes in performance thanks to engineers looking for ground-breaking innovations. In the 1960s, the Cosworth company became the first to use an engine as part of the chassis. In the 1970s, companies such as Lotus harnessed the power of aerodynamics to give their cars an inverted wing shape, drawing them closer to the ground and enabling vastly increased cornering speeds.

In the 1980s, John Barnard, one of Formula 1's greatest innovators, introduced the use of carbon fibre to construct safer, stronger and lighter cars and also dispensed with the gear lever, enabling drivers to keep both hands on the wheel while changing gear with a paddle shift. Mike Coughlan, a renowned designer in his own right, has spoken about how Barnard drove innovation. Each Saturday he would come into the office simply to devote time to alternative approaches and radical thinking. Rather than concentrating on a specific problem, Barnard would step back, look at the fundamentals and create a vision for what came next rather than doing the detailed grind. This approach – taking time out from routine, operational delivery to focus on fresh thinking – is something all great innovators have in common.

Barnard's successor in the modern era is Adrian Newey who reflects on thirty-five years as an innovator as follows:

'I can look back on an eventful, fruitful career – one spent designing cars and asking myself the same series of simple questions. How can we increase performance? How can we improve efficiency? How can we do this differently? How can I do this better?'[41]

In a world of volatility and hyper-disruption, the ability to innovate is critical to allow organisations to respond quickly. This is why innovation is our seventh principle. Barriers to entry in any market and industry are at an all-time low and differentiation can quickly become normalised. Any new product rides a wave of differentiation. After the big fanfare when the new product launches, its unique features soon become the baseline. Consumer expectations grow and, with that, your differentiation starts to disappear. You have to embed a cycle of constant innovation in your organisation to stay one step ahead of the competition. In Formula 1, this week's innovation that gives you a competitive advantage can be copied and normalised by the competition in time for the next race. The cycle of continual innovation is key.

There are also many myths about what makes innovation work and why it fails. In this chapter, we bring together our experiences across different industries to dispel those myths and give examples of innovation that can make a difference.

The innovation myth

Hero innovators like Steve Jobs are rare. They are so rare that they have iconic status. Organisations must find different ways to make innovation work for their business, rather than relying on one individual's charisma and personality. The reality is that innovation in 99% of businesses does not happen like that. A big idea does change things, but there are other contributing factors. Often, it is teams made up of different roles, capabilities and cognitive diversity that convert an idea into reality. Organisations that recognise and respect the contributions of this broader, diverse set of people, and not just the innovation heroes, achieve a competitive advantage.

It is rare to find an innovation that is totally new and unique. The ideas that work – the award-winning inventions – are reinventions. The iPhone, for example, is just a telephone. It makes calls and sends text messages, but many different people at Apple have enhanced it to give the iPhone its competitive advantage. Tesla has done the same. At its simplest level, a Tesla is a car that you can drive from A to B, just like any other, but Tesla has thought differently about the buying, driving, fuelling and service experience. This gives Tesla a competitive advantage and a white space it completely owns. Most engineering discoveries would never become successful products without the contributions of other scientists or engineers. Successful innovation comes not only from within your organisation but also from outside contributions. Every major invention is probably the result of contributions from people around the world that you may never meet. These people never win awards.

Innovation relies on people collaborating and building ideas. It is an incremental and cooperative enterprise based on the commercial reality of the contributions of other inventors, innovators and investors rather than a single hero. There is a risk that we believe that only creative gurus can be innovative and that the rest of us can't contribute, but we need micro-innovation at all levels for all people. The last 100 years have been about efficiency. The world's most efficient companies are rarely the most innovative. The whole business model and economy have been built on trying to make things the most efficient (to increase stakeholder value). High efficiency and standardisation are not a good breeding ground for innovation.

Why innovation fails

Innovation must be nurtured. The best ideas are cultivated over time and often fail many times before they finally come to fruition and become a success. This happens because of a lack of market orientation. We discussed the arrogance of expertise in Principle 6 (talent), where only those who know their customers can develop products that inspire enthusiasm and set themselves apart from the competition. You can only deliver innovative products by having a deep understanding of your customer. In our experience, many organisations neglect customer analysis and customer insights. They do not talk to their customers and have limited access to useful customer information. Much of what they deliver is assumption-based. They think they know their customers because they have been part of the organisation for so long. Organisations that do talk to customers may only do so during the sales process and not during the service process. If you design out the need to contact to minimise a product failure, you are never going to have a meaningful dialogue with your consumer.

A satellite telecoms client we worked with had great customer service during the installation process but did not monitor the quality of the service experience afterwards. When they did finally look at this, it was clear that there was a huge gulf between initial customer satisfaction when the satellite service was installed and satisfaction with the service day-to-day after that. This resulted in them shifting their emphasis far more towards the in-life service experience rather than focusing on installation.

Organisations need to value data and insight more than they value expertise or domain knowledge. Every decision you make to optimise your products and services must be driven by insight and that insight needs to be informed by customer behaviour.

Data is important and yet often neglected. If you create new products based purely on data, there's a risk that you design for things that happened in the past. The organisations that win also think about and anticipate future needs. Success in innovation comes from combining both customer insight and data to anticipate what future markets and future needs might be. Those patterns may not exist in the data sources you have today. Building true customer centricity within your organisation is key. This includes thinking about future generations. The way fourteen-year-olds interact with their friends today will inform the type of service they may want from you when they are twenty-one, but organisations often do not talk to potential customers until they become customers. The organisations that start to talk to customers before this will plan for their future needs. That's where you start to become a more futurist business rather than an organisation that is data-driven only.

Time and time again, organisations are seduced by new technology and deploy it without understanding the role they want it to play or the value they want it to enable. The customer experience that sits over the top is missed out. Technology provides logic, features and functions that enable you to do something. It is the customer experience that makes the difference. In our experience, the most successful innovations are small tweaks to customer journeys and continued leveraging of legacy technology. Technology for the sake of technology has never transformed anything. Organisations can tie themselves up in long-term transformations that cost hundreds of millions of pounds at a time and deploy new capabilities that serve little purpose.

Amazon did not invent e-commerce. They created a slick e-commerce experience that is an exemplar for everyone else. Uber did not create taxis. They created an easy way to get a taxi to come pick you up right where you are. Technology in both of these examples doesn't make the difference; the differentiator is the customer experience that sits over the top.

Generation Z has grown up documenting every meaningful life experience on social media. They have different buying habits from other generations. They want experiences – travel and events, for example. They are less concerned about physical products such as cars and clothes. If the experience is the new product, organisations that want to be successful must innovate with a focus on that customer experience. Retailers are now creating compelling in-store experiences to make their stores a destination that consumers want to go to. They go there because they can document their experience. This is the same with restaurants. How often do you see young people on social media standing in front of an experiential feature, such as a wall of flowers, in a restaurant? Innovation has to be about designing differentiation through experience.

The fragility of innovation

Big ideas and innovations rarely arrive with fanfare. They become successful over time. The journey they take on their path to greatness is often uncertain. They can be met with scepticism and often crushed, ignored or neglected when they first hit the market.

Ideas must be nurtured but organisations think that the power of the innovation will help them blast

THE FUTURE BUSINESS FORMULA

through any obstacle or barrier. This is a dangerous mistake to make. The reality is that when you have the seed of an idea, the result will probably look very different to when you started. Your initial experiments are likely to fail. It is going to take multiple iterations, building on the first idea, to find a version that lands with customers. If you believe in the idea and you have insights that show that it is worth pursuing, then you have to nurture it.

The concept of the 'false fail' connects with the fragility of innovation. Ideas will fail but often the idea itself is not flawed. If you test ideas and concepts with the wrong segment or the wrong demographic, they may fail. It's important to be clear about who the target audience is. Many organisations try to target a new type of consumer but take products and services they have always delivered to a different type of consumer and find that they fundamentally fail when they test them. It does not necessarily mean that the product or service that they are selling today is no longer fit for purpose. It was simply more suitable for a different demographic and a different type of consumer.

It is key that organisations are intentional about who they are targeting and who they are not. Friends Reunited and MySpace both existed before Facebook and failed because of poor user experience. As people's expectations and needs changed, design, usability and experience became more important to them – Friends Reunited and MySpace did not move with the times.

Facebook, on the other hand, took an idea and simplified it to the point where it became easy for people to adopt. This is a classic case of reinventing ideas that came before.

Ingredients to make innovation work

The following ingredients are important to make innovation work:

1. People must be able to challenge the status quo. Most organisations do not encourage this. They do not look at their competitors (traditional and non-traditional), they do not talk to their customers and they do not look at the world around them. An outside-in view of the world is key to making innovation happen.

2. If you have an organisation full of completer-finishers, innovation will struggle. They will want everything to be perfect, which conflicts with the dynamics of experimentation and creativity.

3. Leaders need to create the right environment for innovation. This includes making the time for blue-sky thinking, being curious, making sure resources are allocated to innovation (whether that's time, people or money) and embracing unconventional ideas and thinking from the people they hired to do that.

4. Systemising innovation is the key to success if you want to create new products or new product strategies to stay ahead of the competition. Unless you can consistently deliver those products to customers on time, on budget and to specification at the right quality, you will be beaten by the competition. You must systemise and balance radical innovation with operational excellence. The two things go hand in hand. You can't have an organisation full of mavericks and creative people and, equally, you can't have an organisation full of those who are brilliant at running the franchise. You have to recognise that the two are complementary and find a balance. The key to success is to build a bridge between the two so that they understand and respect the role each plays. Focus on the systems and the processes that embed the patterns you need to make innovation work.

Many of these ingredients touch on the principles we have talked about in previous chapters such as not forcing people to work inside the system, allowing your innovators to work outside the system and allowing them the freedom to be creative.

This is important when it comes to emergent strategy which we talked about previously. Amazon did not decide that overnight they were going to move from being a bookseller to the number one cloud service provider in the world. They navigated a path that gave them scope to sell those products and services. They understood their customers and knew where they had permission to play. Taking small steps, they grew those relationships and created adjacent opportunities. It is impossible for an organisation to make a seismic leap from its core business to a completely new business overnight. We saw this when Microsoft tried to imitate Apple by creating its version of the iPod. The reality was it did not have permission to do this because no one saw it as a provider of music players. Many people say the Zune was a better device than the iPod but, without permission from Microsoft's customers to play in that space, it failed. Microsoft was a computer software company, not a hardware company, whereas Apple had hardware and software from the beginning. Apple also invested early in its Apple Store, which Microsoft did not have an equivalent of.

We have seen similar with mobile phone network operators globally. As the mobile proposition became commoditised with unlimited minutes, data and texts at the cheapest price point, operators built large customer bases with lots of data. Mobile operators have been trying to upsell products and services to their customers which have largely received pushback because consumers only want them to deliver minutes, data and texts as cheaply as possible and ensure that those services are reliable. Customers look to the handset and app makers for innovative content and services.

Mobile operators should not try to be the new Facebook or WhatsApp because those providers will always do it better than they can. They need to scale back their operations to protect their margins. They need to accept that this is the natural life cycle of business. Eventually, services become normalised. Minutes, data and text are no longer a differentiator. Providing the iPhone is no longer a differentiator. Everybody has it. Customer loyalty pivots away from the network providers to the experience of the actual device and consumers can take that device anywhere. The customer relationship shifted from the provider to the mobile device, and the products and services

wanted by customers sit over the top of the network connection they provide.

Summary

Leaders need to adapt their mindsets in the twenty-first century to create an environment for successful and continuous innovation. The pirate and punk mentality we referred to in earlier chapters is key to

encouraging people to think outside of the system that most are forced to work within. Creating teams that exhibit cognitive diversity is key. Most innovation is recombinant – the bringing together of different ideas that create something new. You need to create an environment where 'idea sex' can happen to create new ideas. Value the knowledge and capabilities within your teams and the insights they bring to the table irrespective of where they sit in the organisation. This is key to finding those breakthrough ideas in unexpected places.

Actions to take

1. Innovation is mostly from collaboration and augmentation. You must create an environment that nurtures this. You don't need innovation heroes; you need idea sex.

2. Make data and insight more important than opinions.

3. Innovation is a foreign body to bureaucracy. Make space for the 'artists' in your organisation by removing their constraints.

4. Innovation needs to be executed. Create systems and scalable patterns to accommodate the 'soldiers' you need to produce your ideas.

8

Principle 8 – Change And Delivery: Deliver Small Packets Of Value Regularly

Pit Stop – non-negotiable deadlines

The need to bring a new product to market each year and deliver performance upgrades to that product across a World Championship season that comprises twenty-three Grand Prix means that Formula 1 teams must be focused on delivery. Meanwhile, the competitive and regulatory environment means that change is ever-present. The requirement to build a new car that passes the mandatory compliance tests by an agreed deadline means that there is an inherent sense of urgency to meet twenty-three non-negotiable deadlines throughout the year.

In effect, these organisations have to deliver real, measurable value every two weeks. This creates an environment where the whole team has to embrace constant evolution and change. Since every person and department is living through micro-changes daily, the prospect of larger changes is less daunting. Formula 1 teams understand that, faced with a major shift in technology, regulation or economic conditions, their inbuilt trajectory of evolution and change will ensure that they rise to meet those challenges.

If delivering new value every two weeks is Formula 1's mindset, asking companies to achieve it every ninety days is reasonable. Within Formula 1 teams, the change agents – the innovators tasked with driving continuous improvements in product performance, operational delivery and execution – combine their expertise to focus on a range of problems, large and small, and create the solutions and outcomes that will help the team achieve its goals.

The 'glass tube', a concept that will be discussed in more detail later in this chapter, is present in Formula 1 teams in the form of innovation working groups – small teams of people, sometimes informally structured, from across the business – tasked with challenging established ways of doing things and upending conventional wisdom. They focus on getting solutions live, testing them and securing feedback.

When Red Bull Racing and Renault came up with a way to use the car's engine to pump large volumes of air into key aerodynamic devices, even at low speeds, it produced a step-change in performance which helped pave the way for four years of domination.

Technical director Adrian Newey had his own approach to trying new things and creating more value and exported that approach to his entire organisation. Through continuous communication and rapidly prototyping potential solutions, everyone in the team can appreciate that there is a restless curiosity to improve. 'I'm accustomed to having ideas all the time,' wrote Newey in *How to Build a Car*, 'on planes, in the loo, in the dead of night. They come thick and fast, sometimes at inopportune moments.'[42] Newey goes on to say that even if they're not great, especially those dead-of-night ideas when he wakes up thinking he's cracked it and scribbles something down that by morning looks like absolute rubbish, at least he is generating ideas, which the first step in the process.

Newey's approach to leading a team is normative. Collaboration is central to ensuring outcomes that work and motivating everyone to contribute to the solutions they are seeking. Individual ideas and creativity are brought together and diversity of thought combines to drive solutions to seemingly insoluble problems.

It is thanks to this approach that the Formula 1 industry has been able to pivot quickly when faced with existential challenges caused by economic cycles, legislation, disruption to its channels to market or new consumer behaviours. Experimentation is to be encouraged and risk is not a bad word. The take-away is that when teams of experts try new things and play to their core strengths, surprising outcomes emerge that can be scaled into profoundly positive business outcomes.

In this chapter, we will discuss the eighth principle of the Future Business Formula – change and delivery. Delivery models of the past are no longer fit for purpose in the unrelenting pace of today's world of hyper-disruption. The barriers to entry in most markets or industries are low because the cost of doing business is at an all-time low. Yet, methods for change are often designed in a linear, sequential way that packages lots of things together into large projects and programmes. The time to value is too long, making it hard for organisations to solve urgent problems. Organisations must think about delivery and change in a different way and be highly adaptive to dramatically increase their speed to value. The world is more exponential now than it has ever been which contributes to the problem. Change is higher on the agenda than ever before because of that.

Successfully managing the complexities of today's changing environment requires a new approach that helps CEOs and executive leaders equip the workforce to become adaptive, resilient and effective, reduce risk, improve business outcomes, and create genuine value for shareholders and stakeholders. The ability to deliver small packets of value regularly can hack the old delivery system to great effect.

The volatile world - VUCA

VUCA stands for volatility, uncertainty, complexity and ambiguity. It is a military term that has been adopted in today's ever-changing business world. The training and scenario-planning involved in the response to VUCA gives us insights into how to work in this environment. Military teams train and scenario-plan knowing full well that the plans often go out of the window once they are on the battlefield, but how they train will help them adapt to almost any situation. The business community can learn a lot from thinking about VUCA and how to respond effectively to it.

Organisations formed fifty years ago were built for efficiency using structure and reductionism. It was assumed that as things went down the production line, they would add up to form something coherent at the end. That old model is irrelevant in the new knowledge age. Worse than that, it's holding organisations back. Not only do structures need to change but also the way we do delivery. Unfortunately, today, we often do not know what or how to build it, having never built it before. This moves us from a complicated environment to a complex one. Models such as the Stacey matrix and the Cynefin framework are useful in helping us to understand and make sense of complexity and therefore the type of response and leadership required.[43,44] The way we do change and delivery must adapt to that shift, but many organisations have not changed or are struggling to change.

Although most organisations run projects and programmes of some form, change as a capability has largely been commoditised. Change management is outsourced to HR. Project management is viewed as a skill that is defined by certification and technical developers are often viewed as a factory of battery hens where we drive to the lowest cost possible. The value the organisation places on the people it hires to deliver change has massively diminished. Change is one capability where low cost means low quality. We see this in many organisations that outsource to places like India where the cost of doing change is significantly lower. Yet change and delivery are essential capabilities required for the modern organisation to thrive. This is not an area of cost on which to skimp. We need to shift our view of change from an activity focus (sporadic, turbulent, when needed) to a capability focus (continual, normalised, inherent). Organisations need to become continuously change-ready.

We advocate a new approach in which you focus on the quality and expertise within your organisation's change function. Do not prescribe what they do but focus them on outcomes and trying to solve a problem. You'll find expertise starts to emerge in unexpected places and your ability to deliver value significantly increases. This is important as it allows you to shift towards delivering outcomes rather than outputs, using data and insight to truly focus on the customer and move the strategic dials. New ways of working that are right for your organisation emerge, evidenced by the value that has been delivered. We find that improved employee engagement then comes for free.

Many organisations have been successful over previous decades through size and efficiency but they are now being overtaken by organisations that are nimble. If you want to be effective in the modern world, you need to be nimble and fast. Trying to use size and efficiency to compete is no longer enough.

Deliver value every ninety days

The average time that an executive spends in most organisations is about three years. They succeed or fail in an organisation by their ability to hit their numbers. As we have said, when driving change to deliver a commercial outcome, grow customers or improve customer service, most organisations use large-scale transformation as a vehicle for change. This often fails because the organisation runs out of patience. We must think differently about how to design and deliver change. We advocate finding ways to deliver meaningful value every ninety days (minimum). Rather than delivering large and complex change over three years, the challenge should be broken down into smaller delivery components. This helps people see the transformation happening daily. The executives can connect the dots between business as usual and the transformation because they are serving a business right now and not deferring the benefit to some point in the future when they may not even be in the organisation. We want to take organisations on a journey from delivering value annually to delivering value every ninety days to eventually delivering value every day.

To get to a point where you are delivering value every day, we use a concept called the 'steel thread' as a foundation stone for transformation. Think of it as a tracer bullet that runs through the problem you are trying to solve. You may want to deliver many things over three years, but can you find a steel thread that runs through everything that will deliver value in its own right? Can you find a way of deploying that within ninety days? It could be one customer journey or service, for example. By delivering that customer journey into production, you begin to put up the scaffolding for a technology platform. If a bank deploys the collections journey in ninety days, the architecture needed to support that journey is the same as the architecture that supports every other journey. Therefore, you can get the scaffolding in place for one journey within ninety days, quickly iterate around it and start to build other services. Most organisations, though, try to design and build all their journeys, services, reporting and data before they push any of that into production.

By taking a ninety-day approach, you can strive to make change happen every day. The infrastructure is there to allow you to create small, isolated microservices quickly, creating new experiences and iterating on customer journeys. This approach accelerates getting value out the door. The best way for organisations to embed new delivery patterns and deliver value in ninety days is by establishing what we call an exemplar team. This is a team that can demonstrate the new ways of working. They do that in what we call a 'glass tube'. We create a figurative protective layer of glass around the team to prevent other people from interfering and trying to slow them down. The point is that it is highly visible and you can see into it but you can't access and disrupt it.

We do this because it is difficult to prove that agile (or any modern way of working) can succeed if you are trying to do too much at once. The S&S glass tube

approach focuses on one discrete area of your portfolio and allows a narrow and deep immersion into agility and modern delivery methods. Only when the new ways of working have been created, stabilised and shown to be effective in the right context do we advocate that you consider replicating them as you scale.

The team is set a mission and we pull all the capabilities that they need to execute that end-to-end into the glass tube. We use some key roles in the glass tube to catalyse new approaches and concepts. We also instil data and insights at its core to facilitate data-driven decisions. The team then identifies key valuable changes they can deliver by running a short intensive inception phase lasting a few weeks.

The S&S glass tube allows everyone to see what the team is doing but prevents them from disrupting the work. We ensure that the work they are doing is meaningful and complex enough that the resulting patterns that emerge can be reused elsewhere. That is why we advocate that they bite off something difficult. If you can make it work on the most complex and most important thing, you can do it anywhere in your business.

The key is how people learn. If we think about the learning pyramid, we know that knowledge retention following passive learning (reading something, attending a training course or watching a video) is poor – maybe 5–20% after two weeks. The S&S

glass tube uses kinaesthetic or participatory learning (learning by doing). By observing an expert, doing it alongside them and discussing, coaching and pairing, we know knowledge retention rates soar to 50–70%. We can increase that knowledge retention to 90% if we inform people that afterwards they will be expected to teach others (their peers). This prompts the brain to learn in a different, more effective way. As the great systems thinker, Russell Ackoff, said, the best way to learn something is to teach it.[45]

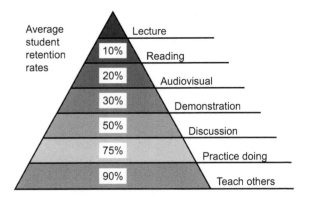

The Learning Pyramid adapted from Edgar Dales' Cone of Learning

While in the glass tube, the team needs to be highly visible at the centre of the business to become an exemplar. We promote using ceremonies that are open to anybody with an interest to attend. That could be to show their planning games, their retrospectives, their showcases, or whatever is of interest to the organisation. Only those who are named as a sponsor or stakeholder or are in the team itself can speak or ask questions at those ceremonies. A large audience will watch what is going on and observe the new ways of working but, because of the theoretical glass tube, they are prevented from asking disruptive questions unless they have a vested interest in what the team is doing. We find this creates interest across the business. Humans are masters at social copying. People begin to mimic what they see in the glass tube. We like to think we are all individuals but, in reality, we like to fit in and conform. By being an engaging place to work, delivering value and creating better ways of working, the rest of the organisation gets curious and starts to pull ideas and concepts from the glass tube into their work. The delivery lead ensures the team communicates constantly about what they are doing through video, blogs, face-to-face meetings and stakeholder meetings to demonstrate the new ways of working. The learning experience becomes as important as what is being delivered.

The bonus of this approach is the engagement from and empowerment of the team. We often see employee engagement surveys 30% higher in the glass tube team than in the rest of the organisation. Critical to making this work, though, is that the sponsor of the work needs to be a senior leader in the business. Their job is to protect the team and enforce the boundaries to ensure there is no disruption. They do this by being part of a guiding coalition.

The guiding coalition

A guiding coalition is a cohort of the best people in an organisation that come together to sponsor and guide change. The coalition consists of a relatively small number of people led by one member of the senior executive team. Not all of the executive team needs to be involved. The coalition must be powerful and have influence, but that influence doesn't have to come from status or hierarchy. The coalition's role is to develop a compelling vision of the future state, set the glass tube team's mission and communicate it to customers, stakeholders and employees. They remove obstacles to successful delivery and they empower the team but they do not prescribe their work. They only remove the barriers and resolve the challenges that are likely to derail success. The guiding coalition does not have to be the most senior people. It has to be the best people in the business, irrespective of their job title, status or tenure, to ensure that change is a success. They tend to be highly connected influencers in the organisation.

Code beats paper

Organisational change can take a long time because so much time is spent upfront on building architecture, designing, planning and prioritising. We advocate finding that steel thread, writing code (or making change) and getting going. That way you can give people tangible results quickly. Deliver a prototype

A Formula One team's work consists of small regular improvements. It's not one big bang project.

and don't waste time doing theoretical design work because there's no substitute for getting real-time feedback from the end user to determine how your design should develop.

We advocate emergent architecture, emergent design and emergent strategy, which are then informed by real-time feedback. This is why the steel thread is important – we are looking at delivering the earliest usable product (EUP) as quickly as possible. Another concept organisations like is the minimum marketable product (MMP) which is the minimum scope required to allow you to market the product to customers. Pushing it live and selling it this way, you will get compelling feedback. Often, EUPs never go live, they are just tested. Getting things into the hands of consumers quickly is critical. We tend not to use the term minimum viable product (MVP). Nothing alarms business folks more than the thought of something barely alive (viable).

Your business as an operating system

We're all familiar with operating models but organisations looking to embed change as a constant and
deliver significant value every ninety days need to
think of their business as more of an operating system. For the first three months after Amazon launched
Alexa, there was nothing like it in the market – it was
truly innovative. Asking Alexa to give you the weather
was unique, but quickly people started to ask it different questions to which it couldn't respond. Suddenly

the innovation became normalised and consumer expectations radically shifted. Amazon's innovation process kicked into gear, a cycle of constantly innovating and adding new features, riding that normalisation and differentiation wave.

We advocate this approach for businesses too. Treat your organisation internally and your products and services externally like an operating system. It is a fallacy for organisations to think that to stay one step ahead of the competition, they have to launch products and services at scale. One feature could make a difference – that constant process of iteration and improvement, introducing new features and capabilities that keep your products, services and experiences fresh and maintain levels of differentiation.

Principles of agility

Agile is an overused word in business. The original 2001 'Agile Manifesto' consists of four values and twelve principles.[46] It comprises a lot of common sense, but it is not common practice. It is simple, but not easy to do. There are many agile frameworks you can use these days, different approaches that are compellingly marketed, but it's important to remember you have no idea if they will work in your context. The point about agile is you have to apply the values and principles and then work through, sense and adapt, and let the way emerge. There is no right and wrong around agile, despite the war that seems to have appeared among the different factions. The other key thing to remember is that agile is not a magic bullet. It does not fix your problems, but it does expose your problems so that you can work out how to fix them. It also creates complete transparency through the delivery teams which can be uncomfortable for those whose jobs seem to revolve around obfuscation.

Agile values	Agile principles
Individuals and interactions	Satisfying customers
Working product	Changing requirements
Customer collaboration	Delivering frequent value
Responding to change	Daily collaboration
	Motivated teams
	Face-to-face communication
	Progress measurement
	Sustainable work pace
	Technical excellence
	Simplicity
	Self-organised teams
	Continuous improvement

If you're worried that this is just for technology teams, simply replace the word 'software' with the word 'solutions' and it can be used for business teams.

Three types of people change

There are only three ways to help people change. The first is the rational approach. This approach says, 'I'll talk, you listen; we'll do some PowerPoint, some training and some comms.' Most organisations use this approach to change and it works if the proposed change is aligned with people's values. If you want to change something different from someone's values, experience or intuition, they are likely to rebel against it. They feel change is being done to them – they haven't been involved or consulted and it feels foisted upon them. Big upfront design, top-down change and the received wisdom of experts fall into this camp. Some may call this change resistance.

The second way of doing change is a coercive approach. This is not advised as an organisational strategy although some organisations probably do use it. Coercion is about the big stick and the little carrot – the standard approach in organisations where there's a power-driven hierarchy and lots of command and control.

The third way is a normative approach, the principle of which is helping others study the system (people, processes, interactions, policies etc) in front of them. By taking this approach, people study and discover the dysfunction and problems for themselves. The act of personal discovery makes people much more receptive to looking for new solutions.

Most organisations use the rational approach to change which is rarely effective. By taking the normative approach, you are building change on a small scale at first and engaging in a process of discovery together. People feel more engaged and motivated to fix things. They feel they are part of the change and empowered to lead it.

Summary

With the pace of change in the environment, old ways of doing delivery are no longer sufficient for organisations. Coupled with that is the fact that change has been commoditised. Yet, the ability to change and deliver to market has become a critical part of helping organisations adapt, innovate and deliver at speed or, in other words, survive. Formula 1 has built its business model around new delivery every few weeks (it has to be ready for the next race).

The good news is that there are new ways of doing delivery and change that are effective in a VUCA world. Implementing them needs to be done carefully. Top-down, designed upfront is a recipe for change resistance. Moving to an emergent approach that empowers your people to fix their problems works brilliantly. Challenge them to deliver small packets of value regularly. To make it work, the role of the leader needs to change from the familiar command-and-control to one of creating an environment in which others can flourish.

Actions to take

1. The world is VUCA and complexity means a different approach is needed. Take time to understand complexity and how leadership needs to be different in that environment. Learn to sense and respond rather than imposing simple, and often wrong, solutions.

2. Deliver value regularly, at a minimum every ninety days, and work towards daily value delivery. It will feel impossible at first, but it can be done.

3. Read and apply the agile values and principles to as much work as possible. It's mostly common sense. Don't be tempted by pre-packaged frameworks that may not work in your context and will distract you.

4. When thinking about people change, move from rational and coercive to a normative style.

PART 4
HOW WE WORK

The fourth part of this book is about how we work. We have all experienced times when work flows without friction. Everything just seems to click. We have also experienced times when the organisation feels like treacle and getting anything done seems to be buried in process, policy and silos.

Humans are great at working in unproductive ways. We believe we are working logically and intuitively but hand-offs or the wrong incentives are driving behaviours and we lack alignment. This slows us down and makes things much more complex than needed.

We are great fans of agile but agnostic about frameworks. We are not going to tell you how to do agile in this section. There are many sources on the subject and many experts to help. We do recommend that you apply the four values and twelve principles of the 'Agile Manifesto' to your organisation wherever possible.[47] We are going to discuss four areas that will help you create business agility to complement the agile values and principles.

In this part, we will look at:

- Simplification
- Organisational design
- Learning
- Measurement

9
Principle 9 – Simplification: Operate At The Speed Of A Start-Up

Pit Stop – keep it simple

A decade ago, a poorly performing Formula 1 team carried out a staff survey which included one simple question: 'What is our primary purpose?' The management expected the answer to include the word 'winning' in terms of winning races and winning the World Championship. Imagine their shock when the responses included 'to make money', 'to make the boss famous', 'to participate in Formula 1' and 'to score championship points'.

Taken aback, the management called a staff meeting at which the CEO explained that he had failed because the purpose of the team was, quite simply, to win. Winning races meant not only having the potential to win the World Championship, but also higher revenue from sponsors, more merchandise sales, greater profitability, higher levels of investment in R&D and, ultimately, more jobs and stability for the workforce.

In a world of complexity, Formula 1 teams know how important it is to keep things simple when it comes to stating clear goals and focusing on the things that matter – the KPIs which make a difference:

- Performance, in terms of speed denoted by lap time, compared to the opposition

- Reliability because to finish first, first you have to finish

- Safety because, when all else fails, the working environment and race operations must ensure that every employee goes home to their family at the end of the working day

The technological landscape in Formula 1 is extremely complex, using solutions from the worlds of aerospace, automotive and information technology to create the fastest racing cars in the world. That complexity is a given and the experts employed by the teams are fully capable of dealing with the specific technologies being deployed. As experts in their areas, they are empowered to innovate, collaborate and experiment in developing new opportunities and solutions.

The most competitive teams do not burden that already complex environment with strict hierarchies.

They operate as closely networked organisations with short lines of communication between individuals, functions and disciplines to drive a rapid response to problem-solving and ensure alignment across the business in dealing with the things that matter.

Mike Gascoyne, former technical director of major teams including Jordan, Benetton and Toyota, points out that you can create KPIs for everything, listing many targets and forgetting the simple truth that, in the case of Formula 1, the only KPI that matters is contained in the list of results published at 4pm on a Sunday when the race finishes. You win or you lose. The deficit to or margin over the competition is plain to see. There is no point over-complicating matters – he recommends a clarity of focus on the things that will make a real difference and avoiding distraction.[48]

Organisations are diseased. They have become big, ugly and complicated over time. Too much bureaucracy causes organisational bloat which leads to slowness to respond. There can be motion but not much progress. According to Cyril Northcote Parkinson, bureaucracy increases by around about 6% a year and, unless it is being removed at the same rate, your organisation is becoming slower every year.[49] This is avoidable. It is a choice and it has to be addressed to become a future business.

In this chapter, we will discuss our ninth principle – simplification – and how organisations can simplify themselves to allow a faster response and better decision-making that will help them outperform their competitors – to operate at the speed of a start-up, or a Formula 1 team.

The complexity excuse for not delivering

Complexity requires a new tactic instead of the classic approach used by leaders for many years. We are now in a highly connected, VUCA world where cause and effect are often no longer obvious and cannot be ascertained by analysis. In other words, we are no longer in a deterministic world where we can simply plan our way out of things.

Organisations can be unnecessarily over-complicated. Often, that complexity exists because people's jobs need it to exist. It does not add value to the organisation. You can take layers of complexity out of the organisation and it will often have no detrimental impact on the business.

We also need to learn techniques for embracing complexity by using fast experimentation to find out what does and does not work. We can make decisions based on the best information we have at the time and continue learning as we move forward, more like a heat-seeking missile than the carefully planned trajectory of a cannonball. Complexity is often perceived as a reason for failing to deliver and yet it just requires a different approach.

We exist in a complex and unpredictable world. Many organisations look for certainty but little is ever certain. To try to manage uncertainty, they build layers of structure and controls which often compound the problem and slow down communication.

Japanese knotweed of bureaucracy

To understand the bureaucratic problems that organisations struggle with, we have to understand where bureaucracy originally came from. Max Weber (1864–1920), a German sociologist, historian, jurist and political economist, is regarded as among the most

important theorists on the development of modern Western society. His ideas profoundly influenced social theory and social research. Weber was considered the father of bureaucracy and argued that bureaucracy constituted the most efficient and rational way to organise human activity and that systematic processes and organised hierarchies are necessary to maintain order, maximise efficiency and eliminate favouritism. On the other hand, Weber also saw unfettered bureaucracy as a threat to individual freedom, with the potential to trap individuals in an impersonal regime of rule-based, rational control. We are starting to see his biggest fear come to fruition.

In his work *The Theory of Social and Economic Organization*, Weber developed six principles of bureaucracy that he maintained were essential:[50]

1. Task specialisation or reductionism – tasks are divided up into simple routine categories based on functional specialisations. Every employee is responsible for what he or she does best and knows exactly what is expected of them.

2. Hierarchy – several hierarchical layers of authority where each layer of management is responsible for its staff and overall performance. This creates many hierarchical positions as a consequence.

3. Formal selection – all employees are selected based on technical skills and competence, which they get through training, education and experience.

4. Rules and requirements – formal rules and requirements are created to ensure uniformity so that employees know exactly what is expected.

5. Impersonal – these regulations and requirements create distant and impersonal relationships between employees. This has the advantage of preventing nepotism and involvement from outsiders or politics.

6. Career orientation – employees of a bureaucratic organisation are selected based on their expertise to make sure the right people are in the right positions.

These principles were invented for the Industrial Revolution when the world was much simpler. Work could be passed down the production line, the thinkers were separated from the doers and the planning was separated from the action. Our world has changed massively since then. This rational structure has become inflexible and rigid, a sclerosis of the organisation. Bureaucracy involves lots of processes and paperwork for their own sake, which are a waste of time, money and effort. Rules and formalities often lead to delays in decision-making. While employees' technical qualifications are important, focusing on those neglects employees' commitment, dedication, potential and softer skills.

We can intuitively see these principles are not right for today's business, yet they are alive and well in industry.

Today's employees are skilled, not illiterate. Competitive advantage comes from innovation, not sheer size. Communication needs to be two-way, not top-down. The pace of change is hypersonic, not glacial.

Gary Hamel and Michele Zanini created the bureaucratic mass index (BMI) to measure how much operational drag comes from bureaucracy. The numbers are frankly shocking with, according to Hamel and Zanini, an estimated $9 trillion per year in lost economic output.[51] There are unicorns. Some large organisations such as Haier, Morningstar, Nuka Steel, Handelsbanken and Linux Foundation have managed to create bureaucracy-free companies.

In summary, bureaucracy gets everywhere. It grows. It is a management tool left over from 100 years ago. It was useful then but, with today's pace and reliance on knowledge rather than structure, it only serves to constrain organisations. Now is the time to strip out the knotweed and simplify.

Roundabouts versus traffic lights

Usually, management is related to performance management in some way. Let's look at a performance management metaphor from Bjarte Bogsnes, Chairman of Beyond Budgeting, about how traffic performance is managed.[52] One option is the traffic light. A simple setup without sensors based on traffic information that may be years old and controlled by the sequence coded, possibly years ago by someone sitting in an office. Many assumptions are made when we choose traffic lights as a tool. For example, that complex problems (road junctions) must be managed with elaborate rules and structure (eg policies and processes). Therefore, traffic lights have cables, lights, switches, controls and a programme to control the traffic. Another assumption is that people need rules and instructions to function properly as they are fundamentally untrustworthy. We also assume that we need to control and manage every possible scenario with visual triggers, such as lights and arrows, dictating and directing the action. This is one way of managing performance.

Let's think about traffic management another way. An alternative would be a roundabout. It is based on real-time information and controlled by you, the driver at the roundabout. Now the assumptions have changed. We assume people are inherently trustworthy and will mostly do the right thing. Many situations could unfold at the roundabout, but social constructs and human understanding will be able to handle them. Complex problems can be managed with simple guidelines and principles that leave room for judgment (eg in the UK, give way to vehicles from the right and go clockwise until you exit the roundabout).

When we think about which method is more effective, safer and cheaper, the answer is always the round-about. The traffic lights may be easier from a user

THE FUTURE BUSINESS FORMULA

perspective as all they require is passive compliance. The roundabout is more difficult as it relies mostly on agreed values. Luckily, that is something that humans are good at.

This demonstrates the difference between managing performance and enabling performance. Most organisations put in place traffic lights that disempower people and dehumanise work, rather than creating roundabouts where people can make their own decisions based on real-time information and broad guidelines and principles. What organisational constructs are you building: traffic lights or roundabouts?

Simplify to align your business

Organisational silos start at executive board level. We have discussed in previous chapters how these leaders are incentivised in different ways and this is where silos begin. As we mentioned in Principle 4 (leadership), leaders need to recognise that it is their job to serve and remove barriers and obstacles. When these roles are ceremonial and they spend most of their time with each other in the executive corridor having lunch, they are not dealing with the issues that are fundamentally impacting the success of their business. Sometimes systemic issues can only be fixed by people with broad influence. Those on the front line feel helpless and at the mercy of the system.

Many organisations are structured and managed traditionally where, rather than leadership teams being aligned around a common purpose, they have their own individual goals. Their functions are often run as separate business lines and are incentivised in a way that drives competition rather than collaboration.

To get a leadership team aligned behind a common purpose and KPIs, you have to remove functional barriers. This is a theme that runs throughout this book. Removing silos and simplifying the agenda puts a laser focus on what is most important to the organisation rather than what is important to an individual. Often, this is the most important five or six strategic drivers or KPIs. Everyone then works out what capabilities and expertise they have to deliver on that strategy.

With this approach, performance management changes too because performance is measured against those important outcome-based KPIs rather than individual contributions or pet projects that add no value. It creates clarity of purpose and defines what success looks like.

Here we need to think about the minimal process and policy we can put in place that will allow an organisation to function but not constrain how people do things. It often takes a long time to sign off something that has little value. Many policies and processes are created to control the 1% of people who might take shortcuts and abuse the principle and this ends up constraining the other 99% of people who are trying to do their best. Therefore, policy and process can sometimes be used as a proxy for management. Wouldn't it be better to ditch many policies and processes and give people flexibility and guiding principles to help free and empower them, and then properly manage the 1% who abuse them? We are all guilty of creating complex processes and policies but we need to re-engineer for the minimum usable process, creating roundabouts in organisations to generate speed.

Rather than spending a long time assessing something on paper, we prefer to get in and find out whether or not it will deliver value through experimentation. At a large international bank, we spent eighteen months trying to get buy-in for a new digital credit card platform, forced into a process that insisted on months of designing architecture and trying to work out the benefits and delivery model. We were watching the birth of a new monolith. We made a breakthrough by securing a small investment to build a prototype in a sandbox. This was a skeleton of the platform in an experimental environment that enabled us to demonstrate new delivery patterns and the value the organisation would get from the investment it was being asked to make. This meant we could validate that the solution made sense and everyone could see and feel the impact it would have on customers and the organisation. It was truly transformational. If we hadn't gone through the process of demonstrating the value that it could add in a low-cost and low-risk way, we would never have achieved approval to build out the platform in production.

Valuing delivery over process is a way to cut through the red tape and get to the heart of what is going to make a difference for your business. Be aware, the status quo is strong and it will fight back, trying to reject any new initiative that shortcuts it. In a complex world, experimentation is the only way out of the analysis paralysis.

Decision-making in a complex world

How we make decisions is dependent on our environment. If it is an ordered, simple environment where cause and effect are fairly obvious and there's only one solution, then we can choose best practice and make the decision based on our experience and intuition. If we are in a complicated environment where cause and effect are linked but not immediately obvious, we can use our experts to analyse the problem and come up with good practice options. When things are complex, when cause and effect are not linked and only obvious afterwards, we need to rely on experimentation as a way forward. Human nature, though, is to favour seeing everything as if it were simple and we use experience and intuition to try to solve issues. Hence our attempts fail or simply move the problem elsewhere. It takes good leaders to do something different and help create an environment where experimentation will eventually find a solution. They have to admit to and embrace complexity, knowing that they do not have the solution themselves. It requires leaders to allow experimentation and see what works and what doesn't. Decision-making in most organisations is poor because decisions are often based on a set of assumptions about what we think customers might want or what might happen in the future. But you only have to look at Kodak or Blockbuster to know that this can be the wrong approach. They assumed that digital technology would never catch fire, and therefore did not pursue it. They couldn't have been more wrong.

Organisations need to accept that the world is changing quickly. The art of decision-making lies in adaptability and this is where experimentation becomes powerful. We need to recognise that many decisions are inter-connected and have consequences in other parts of the organisation. It can be hard to isolate the impact of some of the decisions you make, but breaking deci-sions down into small experiments to test, learn and adapt is a sure-fire way of managing the risks.

To make good decisions, bring a collective of experts around the table. Cognitive diversity is key. At times, it can be hard to reach a consensus and make a deci-sion, which is where you as a leader have to step up to the plate and decide after acquiring a broad set of opinions from the experts. Use as much evi-dence as possible to drive decisions. This is where experimentation will help because you can measure the impact that change is having, which will inform future decisions and demand.

Summary

As an organisation grows, it becomes even more important to keep things simple. Think about the minimum usable process or policies. Implement roundabouts, not traffic lights. Give people guidelines and make decisions as if it was your company. Live the values. You might need some structure but use the concept of organisational scaffolding that can be dismantled easily and reconstructed in new forms rather than building vast functional institutions of granite to celebrate your heritage.

Simplifying your organisation is an ongoing task. It never ends. Policy, process, structures and rules will naturally appear over time, often with the right intentions behind them, but they slow you down. If you have ever worked in a start-up environment, you will know that speed and simplicity are major factors that allow them to be nimble and responsive. Formula 1 is a highly regulated sport with a huge focus on risk. Despite this, they have created an environment where it is also simple for people to make decisions and communicate. Their start-up mentality gives them the agility they need. They have lots of roundabouts.

Actions to take

1. Bureaucracy needs to be stripped out of your organisation at a rate greater than or equal to the rate at which it is being created. This will require continual pruning.

2. Create roundabouts, not traffic lights.

3. Keep your purpose clear and everyone aligned with it. Discuss it regularly. Don't allow silos to form.

4. Embrace complexity and understand that it requires a change in how leaders make decisions.

10

Principle 10 – Organisational Design: Embed An Adaptive Operating Model

Pit Stop – Toyota's strict operating model

Since the start of the twenty-first century, the Toyota Motor Corporation has traded places with the Volkswagen Group as the world's largest car manufacturer, its class-leading Toyota Corolla model a benchmark for large-scale production, quality and cost efficiency.

The Toyota Production System was heavily influenced by the American engineer and professor, William Edwards Deming, whose quality-first approach to improving productivity, reducing costs and increasing market share helped frame the success of the Japanese automotive industry in the post-World-War-Two era. The Toyota Production System is famed for its efficiency, combining lean manufacturing techniques with a relentless focus on continuous improvement. Toyota's management philosophy is known as the Toyota Way – a set of principles and behaviours used by management to drive company performance.[53]

The five key principles are:

- Challenge

- Kaizen (continuous improvement)

- Genchi Genbutsu (see for yourself)

- Respect

- Teamwork[54]

This approach served the company well during the latter half of the twentieth century. When, in 1999, it announced its decision to enter Formula 1, there was a high degree of confidence that Toyota would mirror its successes in car manufacturing with a highly competitive, championship-winning performance at the pinnacle of world motorsport.

After initially delaying its entry from 2001 to 2002, ostensibly to provide the team with a full year of development time, testing and preparation for the challenges which lay ahead, Toyota competed in Formula 1 for eight consecutive years. With an annual technical budget alone of close to €400 million and a purpose-built facility in Cologne, Germany, housing over 1,000 dedicated personnel, Toyota Racing had everything it needed to succeed. Yet failure lay ahead.

The team never won a single race, finished higher than fourth in the team's World Championship or mounted a serious assault on the overall title. In the wake of the 2008/2009 financial crisis, Toyota retreated from Formula 1 and Akio Toyoda, the company's president and grandson of its founder, apologised for the failure. The head of its motorsports division wept during the press conference in Tokyo, the programme's failure a keenly felt, public humiliation.

Now the head of Audi's motorsport programmes, Allan McNish was one of Toyota's drivers during the initial year of testing and its debut season. McNish said, 'Within the structure at Toyota Racing the few people who had the experience were not empowered to lead. They had a very flat structure, with everything decided in meetings, everyone at the same level and no quick decisions.'[55] McNish explained that in such a large group in which everyone had an opinion, it became impossible to make a decision. It lacked empowered leadership.

Bound into the Toyota Way, the Formula 1 team lacked the agility, decision-making speed and empowerment necessary to deal with the fast-moving regulatory, technical and competitive landscape. The operating model and the principles associated with it dictated the structure, with command and control unable to allow for the degree of adaptability required to compete at this level.

Mike Gascoyne, technical director from the end of 2003 until early 2006, confirms in the same article that the operating model developed in the slower-paced environment of volume car production struggled when faced with the white heat of a fast-paced, competitive arena: 'We had a very talented group of people with the budget and facilities necessary to do the job well, but the management structure and its operating principles prevented the team's potential from being unlocked.'[56]

If you saw a car from sixty years ago or a phone from forty years ago, it would be instantly recognisable as outdated, but an organisation from 100 years ago? It would have a familiar organisational chart and a functional structure, reward and punishment as motivators, individual performance evaluations and department goals, and lots of bureaucracy. It would look almost the same as organisations today. Even though the nature of work has changed immeasurably over the decades, organisations have stoically resisted innovation in management principles and practices. In this chapter, we will discuss our next principle which is organisational design, why this has not changed and, more importantly, how you can change it to become an effective future business.

The industrial era is over

Frederick Winslow Taylor, in his book *The Principles of Scientific Management,* created the structures and management principles of organisations over 100 years ago.[57] Many of his ideas are still seen in organisations today. Taylor is known for his analysis of workflows to improve economic efficiency, especially around labour productivity, as people moved from rural crafts to urban factories.

Firstly, he believed that working by habit had to be replaced by a scientific method to study the work and understand the most efficient way to perform a specific task. Secondly, rather than simply assigning workers to any job, he wanted to match the worker to the job based on their capability or motivation and train them to work at maximum efficiency. Thirdly, their performance had to be monitored and supervised to ensure that they were using the most efficient ways of working. Lastly, the work should be allocated between managers and workers so that the managers spend their time planning and training, allowing the workers to perform their tasks efficiently.

As an example of Taylor's initiatives, he noticed that the women in a particular typing pool faced the window where they could see their manager. Once the manager moved out of sight, they became less productive. To solve this, he turned their desks away from the window so that they never knew when their boss was watching them. This improved their productivity greatly. This may sound draconian but, just recently, some big companies have started to implement desktop spyware to monitor their staff while they are remote working. This Big Brother approach is left over from 100 years ago even though the world of work has changed massively in that time.

Niels Pflaeging, in his 2014 book *Organize for Complexity*, illustrates how the industrial environment has changed over time.[58] Up until the 1870s, we were in the age of crafts manufacturing with local markets and high customisation. Value was created by humans – the local blacksmith or similar. In the industrial age between the 1870s and the 1970s, Taylor's principles abounded. We had wide markets, low density, high standardisation and little competition. Taylorism was ideal for this era and value was primarily created by the machine. From about the 1970s onwards, in the knowledge/information age, the world changed again with globalisation and crowded markets with high density, customisation and strong competition. Now we are back to value creation by humans rather than the machine. Even though the world has changed, the now inappropriate legacy management structures and principles are dragging on into the twentieth and twenty-first centuries. We are seeing the limitations of those kinds of structures.

In 2000, the top four companies were industry leaders – General Electric, ExxonMobil, Pfizer and Citigroup. Twenty years later, the top four are digital platform companies – Apple, Alphabet, Microsoft and Amazon. These powerful digital platforms have the scale and scope to expand into new markets. This shows that fast-moving companies, with completely different business models, have been able to accelerate past the traditional, sizeable, efficient organisations of the past.

Forget hierarchy?

Successful organisations in the twenty-first century are built on knowledge, ideas and the ability to differentiate and innovate. They need new structures and ways of working. We advocate collapsing layers and the traditional organisational silos and, instead, bringing together networks of teams with the capabilities you need to solve complex problems and achieve outcomes, rather than passively asking people to complete tasks. You have to recognise that, irrespective of level, people are experts. The person who cleans your office is an expert at cleaning. The person who cooks your lunch is an expert at cooking. The person who builds your software is an expert at building products. Developing this melting pot of expertise and capabilities is the best way to drive innovation and success rather than grouping them into functional silos and teams.

Instead of creating a hierarchy, create an adhocracy and remove rigid bureaucracy by creating flatter structures. These need to be fluid and flexible because we are in an unpredictable world. A rigid organisational structure will prevent you from adapting, innovating and reinventing when you need to.

Technology has been democratised so much that you could start a business tomorrow at a low cost and launch products and services that start to steal customers away from well-established incumbents. Reacting requires the ability to spin up small teams of highly capable people with a melting pot of competencies and expertise. These teams have little formalisation; consequently, you do not prescribe the target operating model. They are allowed to self-form and work out for themselves how to get the best out of each other. The policies that govern the way they work will be lightweight and loose. They are grown-ups and they should be empowered to find the right path to solve the problem.

It is important to note that flatter structures work well in start-ups and organisations up to a certain size, but they struggle beyond Dunbar's number (about 150 individuals) so the size of the groups that work together needs to be constrained to maximise effectiveness. The important message here is that hierarchy done badly is really bad. Hierarchy needs a fundamental shift to relationship power rather than position power. We all know that power corrupts. You only have to look at politics. If organisations focus less on the number of people they employ and more on expertise and capability, then they will find that they can do far more at a lower cost with fewer people. This is about minimising the number of people around the problem and giving teams autonomy, respecting their expertise and judging them on their ability to achieve outcomes rather than on outputs. When organisations do not embed that culture, they require more people to coordinate all the activities. They create multiple cottage industries.

Hierarchy is a natural phenomenon. Dominance hierarchies form in many animal species and help stabilise and protect groups, allowing them to thrive. Hierarchy isn't bad in itself, but in the species with the most complex, expressive language and ability to reason (humans), it can become suboptimal when trying to build organisations.

Networks of experts

We are great believers in the team-based organisation. To create fluid teams, you need networks of people with specific capabilities aligned around missions and problems. Often, the best talent is no longer in your permanent workforce. The executive gig economy is teeming with people who want to release themselves from corporate life because of all of the problems we have talked about in organisations today. It is also the reason we talk about becoming a sought-after organisation that talent wants to work 'with'.

These days, blockbuster movies are created using networks of experts. In the old days, studios (Warner Brothers or MGM, for example) used in-house teams and staff and even had film stars attributed to their them. That's completely changed. Now, they decide on the best director of photography they can get or the best sound technician. These people are pulled in on a demand basis to create an amazing film and, at the end of filming, they disband. This model can and should be applied to your organisation. Your best experts are not necessarily in your permanent workforce and you will have to look elsewhere to find them. Hybrid, on-demand expertise is a model that is ideal for the future challenges of organisations.

We need a new type of operating model

Target operating models are in favour at the moment. The word target implies that once you reach it every-thing will be OK. Often, it takes years to implement them and they move the organisation from one sclerotic form to another. As we have talked about throughout this book, pace and complexity are the real challenges. What we need is a highly adaptive operating model rather than a target operating model.

There are usually three structures in an organisation. Firstly, the organisational structure. This tells us who reports to whom for compliance purposes but it does not tell you how the work gets done. Then there is the operating model. Often this is not written down and people in the organisation do not know it. It has just evolved, usually into something bloated and ugly. The third structure is often invisible, the influencers and social network within the organisation. This is how decisions and ideas travel across a business. Who listens to whom?

There can be a temptation to jump to changing the structure first. It feels tangible and impactful. We advise against this. It rarely changes anything about how work gets done while causing emotional pain along the way. We always advise changing the operating model first to establish new ways of working, using the influencer network to spread change. If needed, you can look at structure last to embed and stabilise the new way of working. What usually happens when you get your operating model right is that people care much less about the structure. The primacy shifts from reporting lines to working in value-creating teams. We don't use a classic operating model approach – more on that later.

The sooner we move from rigid organisational structures towards understanding social movements and networks, the quicker we will find highly effective organisations. Our view is that an operating model cannot be written down. Many organisations obsess year after year, writing down how their business runs, how it is structured and what the processes are, but the dynamics of businesses have changed so much that traditional operating models in their current form are no longer relevant.

Given the dynamics of modern business, there isn't time to perfect an operating model and delivery patterns on paper and then find ways to implement them in a business. We promote five principles for an adaptive operating model that allow new ways of working to emerge through exemplar teams in a 'glass tube' incubator environment that embody these principles:

1. Human: organisations should be designed around people, whether they are employees or customers, and what they care about.

2. Frictionless: organisations should be frictionless. This recognises that businesses are dependent on an ecosystem which can be internal and external. Organisations are dependent on an ecosystem of partners to help them to deliver their business model. For that to work well, integration into the ecosystem has to be seamless and easy to minimise friction and disruption.

3. Optimisation: we have to accept that, with the world changing so frequently, business has to constantly improve and never stand still. Switch from projects and programmes to the insight-driven continuous optimisation of products, services and experiences. Focus less on the number of things being delivered and more on the outcomes that matter.

4. Organic: your teams and their purpose should spin up and down, based on the challenges and demands that they are facing. If something is not adding value, challenge whether it should still be a priority. Wind it down and redeploy resources.

Place less emphasis on job titles and departments and more on networks of expertise coming together to deliver value.

5. Modular: independent, discrete, reusable capabilities that allow a plug-and-play approach using well-defined, standardised interfaces to be able to react faster.

This is not an operating model in the traditional sense. It is a set of core principles that should define and govern the way that an organisation runs, taking an emergent approach to bring the patterns that enable these principles to life.

The problem with structure

Structure does not have to be a problem. There are many examples of highly effective and profitable organisations that have a classical structure. It depends on how it is used. Structure can create a sense of order and help with communication. It can create clarity around responsibilities. Structure becomes corrupted when it is used for power, status and control. Hierarchy or structure is not inherently wrong or bad, but it can become fundamentally restrictive for an organisation if used in the wrong way. There is a current fascination with flatter structures, such as holacracy, which also have their problems. You can find out more about holacracy at www.holacracy.org/explore.

Structure was originally created to get people to conform to a set of behaviours and an ideology. In the corporate world, we are dealing with adults yet the corporate workplace tries to teach them new rules and paradigms for how to behave. Nobody turns up to work to do the wrong thing. You hire people because you genuinely believe they have something to offer but, as we assimilate them into the organisation, we force them to conform to a set of boundaries that suffocates their ability to be creative. The radical alternative is to take an anarchic approach where, eventually, the right sort of order will emerge. Boundaries are needed but it's important to create boundaries that are safe for people to operate within rather than regulating what you call them, who they report to and how they do their job. It is hard to ride innovation waves and stop being normalised if you are forced to follow tight bureaucracy and infrastructures. That's why these types of approaches work well in start-ups where they have an impact quickly. The key is to strip out the organisational complexity and bureaucracy.

If you are contemplating a spin-off, try something innovative. Go for it fully. It is a false economy otherwise. British Airways (BA) tried to do this with its low-cost Go airline to compete against easyJet as a budget airline after observing the success of Southwest Airlines. They thought BA's existing infrastructure

could be used to capitalise on economies of scale, but that infrastructure (hierarchy, policies, processes etc) was for a completely different business model and was too expensive and slow to run a budget airline. They never got costs down far enough and eventually sold Go.[59]

Flattening the structure

Usually, there are layers in an organisation – the leadership layer, the general management layer and the execution layer. The general management layer often exists just to tell people what to do and is usually the most bloated part of the business. Organisations need to consider collapsing this structure and shortening the path between the execution layer and the leadership layer. This will reduce the time it takes for information to cascade down from leadership to execution and will result in far more engagement and motivation among those at the coalface. We have experienced a 30% improvement in employee engagement doing this. Attrition levels tend to be lower because of how empowered people feel once they have this clarity of purpose and mission. Performance management changes too – middle managers tend to manage through a set of tasks whereas leaders set missions. Performance via missions is measured by the ability to deliver value, not by the number of things that they deliver through a production line. Communication levels dramatically improve too as messages are often

diluted when they come via middle management to the execution layer. Taking out this organisational complexity results in a clear line of sight between those at the execution layer and the leadership layer.

During the 2020 pandemic, middle management layers became exposed. Organisations realised that, in a world of remote working, middle management's only role was to pass information on to others. By default, structures were flattened without actually removing anyone. They simply bypassed them, leaving teams to talk and collaborate directly with senior people more than they had ever done before. As a consequence, many organisations are reassessing their structure and questioning the role of the traditional middle manager.

Keep the organisation in beta mode

If you are going to change your organisation to remove complexity, how do you design it so that it works? The key is not to design it entirely. Big, upfront design rarely works. It is often designed in a darkened room by executives and consultants who lack the real context from the front line and it ends up being an assumption-based desktop exercise. It looks great on PowerPoint but the hundreds of pages of Level 0 to Level 5 process flows can't be implemented in the real world. Instead, you lightly design it, aiming to continually keep your organisation in beta mode. You are improving all the time and have to be comfortable with ambiguity and change while helping your people to be comfortable with that too. You do not have to be perfect. You can evolve. There just has to be enough design, based on the information and data we have right now, to make the next best decision. If it does not work, roll it back. If it does work, you will have learned new things and can start planning the next move. It is important to build continual improvement into your values, culture and daily work so that it is expected, supported and rewarded.

The organisations that succeed are the ones that can spin up their business models quickly. YouTube is a great example. Its business model and the types of people it needs have changed over the years along with the way the business is run and the way that it monetises its service.

The best businesses are chameleons. They adapt and change based on the way that market and consumer demand shift. You need to always be in that experimentation mode, recognise that it will feel imperfect and be comfortable with that.

Dunbar's number

In the 1990s, anthropologist Robin Dunbar found a correlation between primate brain size and the average size of their social group.[60] Extrapolating the correlation found with primates and based on the average human brain size, he theorised that the limit on the number of stable relationships that humans can maintain is 150 – this is known as 'Dunbar's number'.

Large, complex organisations have multiple spans and layers, forcing their staff to have a significant number of relationships – often beyond 150 – to get things done. When Dunbar's number is applied in a delivery and organisational context, it starts to flatten the structure, remove the spans and layers and enable your organisation to be nimble and agile. It would be interesting to see if there is an optimum scaling pattern where organisations grow to a maximum of 150 people – and then grow further by replication rather than bloating. A bit like the binary fission reproduction of bacteria, rather than growing into a giant bacterium. This is the approach we use in our organisation.

CASE STUDY: TELECOMS RESTRUCTURE

A large telecom company decided to restructure and cut costs, removing 7.5% of its workforce from each department. After a time, the HR director said that they hardly noticed the difference and that they should have gone to 15%. That was how bloated the organisation was. Our advice is always to retain your talent but trim those who are a commodity, turning up every day simply to go through their functional role.

If you focus on the people who have talent and capability, no matter how inexperienced they are, you will find that they step into the void and take on greater accountability. They then become more empowered. That is when you will find expertise emerging in unexpected places. High-performing organisations empower the people that matter rather than suffocate them with bureaucracy and management layers.

Summary

Your management structures and principles are more than 100 years old and they are slowing you down. The only way out is to keep your organisation in beta mode, flatten the layers and strive for structures that deliver cross-functional customer outcomes rather than functional activity. Operating models are important but the top-down, designed upfront style of creating a beautiful target state is out-of-date. Operating models need to be a bottom-up, emergent design to be effective and adaptive. The reason Formula 1 teams are so competitive and fast moving is that their operating model is adaptive. They have no time for rigidity and slowness when their next public product demo is only two weeks away.

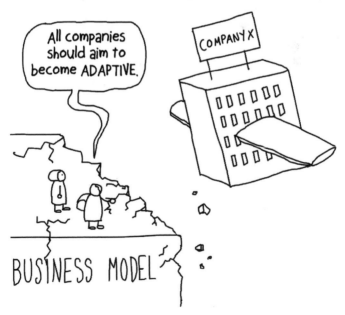

Actions to take

1. Organisational structure can be good for stabilising and embedding a new operating model. If you change structure on its own, you are simply in the business of rearranging the deck chairs on the Titanic.

2. Keep your organisation in beta mode. Fluid not static.

3. Wherever possible, flatten the structure to increase the speed of communication.

4. Create networks of experts in your organisation.

5. Implement an adaptive operating model.

11

Principle 11 – Learning: Bring Diverse Opinions Into The Room

PIT STOP – inbuilt learning

Learning is central to a Formula 1 team's obsession with continuous improvement, the process by which performance is rigorously examined, problems identified and solutions found and implemented at speed. Teams learn by analysing both failure and success and do not hesitate to bring in external expertise to accelerate the learning curve.

In the Netflix show *Formula 1: Drive to Survive* (series two, episode four), viewers were treated to the sight of the all-conquering Mercedes-Benz team having an uncompetitive, error-strewn 'home' Grand Prix, ending with a despondent Lewis Hamilton joining teammate Valtteri Bottas in a post-race debrief with senior engineers.[61] Faced with a poor result, Formula 1's usually dominant team was sitting down to discuss what went wrong and learn from its mistakes. This was nothing new. Learning is built into how they operate. These meetings are held twice a day, every day during a four-day Grand Prix, with all the key stakeholders gathered together to discuss how performance can be improved and issues rectified.

David Coulthard, a thirteen times Grand Prix winner, says in *The Winning Formula*, 'None of us know all the answers, so I believe in surrounding myself with smart people who can deliver the best outcomes for me and help me to keep learning in the process.'[62]

Key to this approach is honesty, openness and transparency, values which all the leading teams have come to recognise as being critical. 'The moment we stop learning we are, in effect, hitting reverse gear,' says Coulthard. 'Learning should not be optional because. . . evolution is an essential and non-negotiable aspect of what we need to do.'[63]

Historically, we would get an education, get a job and then retire. They were distinct phases of our lives. A lot has changed in the last fifty or sixty years. Now, the only way to be successful in business is to be a lifelong learner. We have seen the acceleration and removal of roles quicker than at any other time in history. Roles that were valid ten or twenty years ago have completely disappeared and been replaced by new roles that didn't exist or weren't predicted. That process will continue.

The ability to reinvent yourself through learning has never been more important. If you are not learning, you are standing still. As we said in Chapter 9, organisations are stifled by bureaucracy which, in turn, stifles innovation so much that people end up with learned helplessness. It becomes too difficult to be unique because of that bureaucracy. People switch off their innovation genes and live in the here and now of the dysfunctional system.

How we learn

With the current pace of change, an organisation needs to grow and learn faster than its competitors. That only happens when the people and the employees within it actively learn. The organisation isn't anything if not its people, but most organisations do not take the time to help their employees learn. One of our clients was quite institutionalised. We asked them how they made time for learning. They said, 'We don't really. How would we do that?' We put a plan together for thirty-minute daily stand-up sessions where they researched a particular subject chosen by the leader or by the team. The purpose of this approach was to create the habit of learning and allow time for that to happen. We facilitated the process of applying that new knowledge through experimentation to see what would work.

People assume that you come in to do your job and, if you want to do any learning, you do that at home or on an annual two-day course. The fact is people have busy home lives too and organisations should invest time in learning within the working day.

We want people to consider learning as a continual process and demonstrate a growth mindset, believing that they can get better at what they do by working at it. A fixed mindset will prevent learning through a belief that if you can't make progress in a short time, this isn't for you. It's never as binary as that; we can have both mindsets for different things. Children tend to have a natural growth mindset. It is the leader's job to foster a growth mindset in their employees wherever possible. Part of your role is generating enthusiasm in others.

When we talk about learning, we need to think about soft as well as hard skills. You might want to become a JAVA expert but you should also work on softer skills such as influencing and negotiation in a remote setting. In a distributed workforce where everyone is working from home, there are not the same social cues as in a face-to-face conversation. You should consider building skills to be more influential and effective in this new working model.

People learn in different ways too. In the past, you were given the forty-page company training programme and told to assimilate it. Now we know that people have different learning styles. Some are visual and learn by seeing. They prefer video or graphics. Some are auditory and learn by hearing. They are great listeners, prefer verbal discussions and are good at replaying things. Some prefer learning by doing. These are kinaesthetic learners.

Given these different learning styles, we need to think about how we incorporate body movement, touch and feel, and hands-on application of the work in learning programmes. There will also be generational differences. Generation Z or millennials tend to use short books, blogs or videos whereas Generation X prefer to read and write.

Coaching versus mentoring

We believe that coaching is often more effective than mentoring. Mentoring tends to stroke the ego of the person who is the mentor. It becomes about them passing down their knowledge, experience and wisdom. This can limit learning by the recipient. If the advice the mentor gives the mentee about how to fix their problem does not work, the mentee can lay the blame at the mentor's feet and say they did not know what they were talking about. There may be many reasons why it did not work but mentees can absolve themselves of responsibility by saying that they were given advice that did not work.

Coaching, on the other hand, allows the coach to ask powerful questions to help the coachee become more self-aware about their situation. Coaching takes the coachee to a level of deeper thinking so that they can come up with their own solutions and options. If the coachee tries an option and it fails, they will be unable to blame anyone else because they came up with the options. They own the failure and may have learned new things along the way. The coach can help them assess what went wrong, what new information they have and their other options for action. The coachee will take accountability for the

decision they made. Coaching increases the coachee's accountability for the solution. Learning how to coach (properly) as a management style is something we strongly recommend.

Learning does drive action

There is a hierarchy in learning. Firstly, there is an initial reaction in the person who is learning. Did they enjoy it? Did they engage with it? Did it resonate with them? Secondly, there is an emotional reaction. Did they actually learn anything? Have they taken anything on board? The third level is a behavioural reaction where the person who has been learning puts their new knowledge or skill into practice to drive a different behaviour. This is the outcome we want from learning – that a change in behaviour occurs. There is no change without behavioural change. There is nothing worse than a learning activity being logged as merely interesting, leading to no active change in behaviour. We have to think carefully about the relevance to their existing problems, accessibility to take action, how the learning process happens and how we create an environment in which they can experiment. We need to consider that a rational approach to learning (PowerPoint, training, comms etc) may not work best. A normative approach – studying the problem and the 'system' in front of you, discovering the true dysfunction – is often the best way to help people search out and engage with new ideas.

The arrogance of expertise

As we said in Principle 4 (leadership), those with tenure in an organisation often think they know best, but are they the most important person in the room? Making assumption-based decisions about the types of products and services that your organisation should deliver based on your own opinion is likely to fail. In 1975, a twenty-four-year-old engineer named Steven Sasson invented digital photography while working at Eastman Kodak by creating the world's first digital camera. Kodak wasn't enthusiastic about the industry-changing breakthrough and struggled to see the potential, especially as it didn't align with their core product, photographic film. The eight-pound camera that Sasson put together shot 0.01-megapixel black-and-white photos and recorded them to cassette tapes. Each photo took 23 seconds to create and the only way to view the photos was to read the data from the tape and display it on a TV screen.

Sasson showed the new technology to a number of Kodak executives, but their reaction was initially muted. According to Sasson:

> 'They were convinced that no one would ever want to look at their pictures on a television set. Print had been with us for over 100 years, no one was complaining about prints, they were very inexpensive, and so why would anyone want to look at their picture on a television set?'[64]

At the time, Kodak was the dominant brand in the US photo industry and Kodak didn't want to cannibalise its film businesses. Kodak eventually did make the switch to digital eighteen years later – and filed for bankruptcy in 2012.

Expertise can create amazing communication between two people who have a foundation they can refer to. For two experts, this will feel like a meeting of minds. What if there is a mismatch in that expertise? What assumptions are made when one has expertise and the other person does not? Does it help or hinder? When you teach or need to explain something to someone else, you want to avoid coming across as arrogant or elitist. This is the problem with many experts who wonder why everyone else does not get it. We saw this at first-hand in an organisation we worked with. We led a workshop with a group of experts who continuously talked to the group about what they had done to fix the same problems in other organisations and how they did it. Instead of being well received, it caused barriers to come up and people would not engage with them despite their expertise. The experts failed to recognise this. We saw the body language and quickly changed the approach to the workshop, focusing initially on what everyone could agree about. We asked the experts to stop talking and play a passive role while moving to a much more collaborative, co-creative session with dynamic visualisation of the systemic problems and root causes. People from the incumbent team started to get up and use the whiteboard, leading and drawing in the experts to ask for their opinions when they were needed. They discovered things about their problems they had not seen before and started looking for solutions. Over the rest of the workshop, barriers came down, people opened up and behaviours changed. The original team started to take ownership of the problem, look for new ideas and create solutions.

Radical transparency

The key to increasing learning across the organisation is to improve transparency. Most organisations are incredibly opaque. Leaders can forget that they have most of the context but they haven't told everyone else it. It is a human condition to assume everyone knows what we know, but it causes problems in organisations because many things are hidden. Certain people know certain things, but no one knows the full context. It becomes difficult to make decisions when you only have some of the jigsaw pieces.

When an organisation drives radical transparency across its landscape, people have much more situational awareness and context that allows them to learn more and make better decisions that are more relevant to where the organisation needs to go.

There is, though, the risk that you provide people with so much information that they become overloaded.

You need to provide a level of transparency initially around key things and then provide access to further levels of transparency. Without all of the information, people end up in a bubble trying to do their best based on limited information.

To do this, learning must be made a priority and a learning culture should be built that includes time, investment and resources for learning. It is not enough to simply put people on an annual course. People learn on the job and learn together. Without time for that learning, it is difficult to move forward. One of our clients drove high utilisation rates and a time sheet culture to encourage their delivery teams to be productive but left no time for learning. When we were called in to help them modernise and upskill their technical teams, it hadn't occurred to them that their focus on productivity had stifled learning and ironically slowed them down.

The way to put learning at the core of your organisation is to build self-led learning into personal development plans and job descriptions, hold coaching conversations, create incentive schemes etc and ensure that learning is a two-way process using feedback and feedforward. Don't forget the most powerful factor for embedding cultural values and behaviours we talked about in Principle 5 'what leaders pay attention to'. Want a learning culture? Pay attention to learning. Talk about it at every team meeting. In every one-to-one, ask what they have learned recently. Ask how your direct reports are building learning into their teams. Do it repeatedly and consistently. You don't need HR help or consultants to build your courses. Your teams will do the rest for you – just ask them what they need to make it happen.

Impact of COVID-19 on learning

During the pandemic in 2020, people had to quickly adapt to working in a remote operating model which was enforced on organisations by circumstances. All of the reasons for discouraging remote working in the past disappeared immediately. This process quickly highlighted the areas that added value to an organisation and what did not. For example, the layers of middle management that are recruited to drive command and control, reporting and work allocation found they were no longer relevant. By default, people were forced to work in an empowered and autonomous way.

If that forced change in working practices worked for an organisation, what does that say about the structures and the bureaucracy that have existed for so many years that were rapidly bypassed in a collective effort to remain effective? Many organisations enjoyed new-found freedom from the corporate sclerosis of bureaucracy. How organisations learn from this event will be key: revert to the old ways or embrace the better parts of this new way of working.

They will also need to consider how consumer behaviour has changed and how embedded these new behaviours are. There has been a massive acceleration of the shift to online and a huge drop in the use of cash over contactless, for example. Do not assume that things will return to how they were pre-COVID. Plan as though these new behaviours have become the norm. What does that mean for how businesses will operate? What are the implications for their organisation in terms of the capabilities that they need, how they are structured, how they take products and services to market and how they understand consumer needs and consumer behaviour? Organisations that embrace these changes will succeed. Those that try to buck the trend and drag their consumers back to a pattern and an approach that suits their original business model are likely to fail.

The ability of an organisation to learn quickly from this forced change is key. Some organisations have gone through an existential crisis. They have had to do something fundamentally different during this period otherwise their business would die. They are seeing true transformation in a rapid period and are accelerating past the competition. They are riding the innovation waves now while everybody else that has experience in services is becoming normalised.

Summary

If you are not learning, you are standing still. If you are standing still in the current world, you are going backwards because of the pace of change. Becoming a learning organisation starts with every employee. You have to hire cognitive diversity to prevent blind spots. Only by bringing those diverse opinions together will you start to unlock the real problems you have by looking at them from different viewpoints. Formula 1 teams know this. If you do not have a learning organisation, nothing will fundamentally change. You are simply on a trajectory of hope.

Actions to take

1. For your organisation to remain competitive, everyone needs to be learning. As a leader, you can create a culture of learning by simply paying attention to it.

2. We don't like 'fail fast' as a term, but it needs to be OK to fail (as long as we are learning and improving from it).

3. Create radical transparency to allow people context. When it starts to feels uncomfortable, you are nearly there.

12
Principle 12 – Measurement: Measure What Matters To The Customer

Pit Stop – what matters?

Competing in Formula 1 requires the constant measurement of relevant data to ensure that every system in the car, and every contribution the driver makes to its operations, optimises performance. This is one of the reasons why major technology companies use the sport to create compelling case studies as to how a data-rich environment can be used to transform risk management, performance and the repeatability of positive outcomes.

Following the advent of rudimentary, hard-wired telemetry systems in the 1980s, teams quickly progressed to gathering real-time data through wireless networks. Before this, engineers would use their personal experience, together with insights from asking the driver about car performance, to reach decisions. Much of this was subjective since adrenaline-fuelled racing drivers are not the ideal source of analytical feedback. It also meant that a team's performance depended on a multitude of human factors. The deployment of on-board sensors changed all of that.

It soon became clear that big data was a mountain of information waiting to be mined for golden nuggets, which is where the real value lies. Racing teams want to ensure performance improvement through insights that make a difference – focusing on the key issues concerning reliability, system performance, component life cycle management and driver inputs.

Today a team such as McLaren sells data analytics capability to industry including sectors as diverse as healthcare, infrastructure development and transport. The ability of Formula 1 teams to gain insights from vast data, using predictive analytics to shift gears on the speed and quality of decision-making – including adapting strategies in real time – is at the core of McLaren's application of this knowledge through its technologies division, Applied.

One of the metrics which has been transformed by constant measurement, analysis and insight is vehicle reliability. Between 1950 and 2000, the average reliability of a highly stressed Formula 1 car did not change – 45% of the time cars suffered technical failures, often with catastrophic outcomes including driver fatalities. The use of real-time condition monitoring systems combined with advanced analytics has enabled Formula 1 engineers to build reliability into systems from the outset. A journey of hope has been replaced by a strategy based on deep knowledge and insight. The outcome? Lewis Hamilton's Formula 1 car did not suffer a single failure in 2020. In four years, his complex, 220mph piece of advanced technology only suffered a single failure, due to a minor system error which the team was unable to rectify remotely and they called a halt to operations before any damage was done.

Data-driven insights help achieve the outcomes teams want and avoid those they do not. A perfect blend of performance and risk management based on knowledge. Organisations need to make decisions based on real insights rather than assumptions. This is particularly important for organisations that are delivering services to customers. Assuming what your customers want and how they feel is probably the biggest mistake that an organisation can make.

We are now in a world of data abundance. As human beings, we tend to overestimate the importance of information that we have just encountered or that's frequently repeated. Using gut feeling in decision-making is flawed and unreliable. We overplay our experience and our intuition, assuming that cause and effect are linear and obvious. Many leaders still use gut feeling in decision-making even though they have data available. This could be because they have too much data and do not know what to do with it or they do not have the right insights from that data. In this chapter, we will cover our final principle – measurement. We will discuss what to measure, how to measure and how to use data and insights to drive change and improvements.

What are you measuring?

Recently, we undertook a big multichannel activity for a company. We realised that nearly all of the channel measurements they used were internally focused on the organisation itself. For example, the website response time was green. As were the stock availability, the retail resource schedule, queue lengths and the contact centre response time. When we looked at the multichannel journey for real customers and joined up all the key interactions, we could see huge problems. A customer could order a product online but, if they had a problem with it and took it to one of the company's stores, they would be told that they would have to contact customer services since it was ordered online. Customer services would then say that it wasn't their problem and that the customer needed to go to the website again. If you considered the customer journey as a joined-up and integrated experience, it was clear the performance was red. Yet the company had convinced itself everything was green. Watermelon reporting: green on the outside, red on the inside.

This highlights the problems that occur when there is lots of data but we do not know how to derive useful insights from it. It is rare to see an organisation that drives change demand based on data and insight. It is usually based on the opinion of one or two people who think they know better than anybody else. Insight is critical, turning that raw data into something action-able that you can demonstrate will solve problems and deliver tangible business value.

There has been a shift in recent years with organisa-tions building big data capabilities, data warehouses and event-driven architectures. Event-driven architec-ture is a software architecture paradigm promoting the production, detection, consumption of and reaction to events. An event can be defined as 'a significant change in state'. For example, when a consumer purchases a car, the car's state changes from 'for sale' to 'sold'. Data on its own has no real value because it is subjective. It is one person's opinion on what the data is saying. Building real insights and analytical capabilities that can take all of the inputs and turn them into outputs that become outcomes is critical. Many organisations still have a long way to go to recognise the value of doing that.

Insights are effectively deriving storytelling from data. They get into the heart of the data to translate it into something meaningful. Using data to develop new products and services is better than the highest-paid person's opinion (HIPPO), but many organisations still design products and services based on the views of a product manager or product owner. They assign one person who has been in the organisation for a long time and knows that business inside out. They design products based on what they know about their industry, rather than trying to understand customer behaviour, customer needs and how they are influenced by exemplary experiences in other industries.

Steps to effective measurement

To measure effectively, we need to understand our objective and what factors will help us achieve that objective. Statistics or data need to be consistent and show that the outcome of any one action at any one time will be similar to the outcome of the same action at another time, otherwise, the measurement is unreliable. It also needs to be predictive. There's a cause-and-effect relationship between the action, the statistic measures and the desired outcome.

What you think are your key indicators are probably not. Your data will start to expose what they are. A particular retailer started to measure staff turnover. They realised that they were measuring the wrong thing as this wasn't a predictor of performance in stores. A much better indicator was the turnover of the managers. This shows that, even when we have the data, we still sometimes apply our experience and intuition and think that we are measuring the right thing. We should test whether that measurement is a good predictor and whether it consistently gives you the same repeatability.

In our experience, most businesses will measure everything and end up with too much meaningless information. Instead, think back to the steel thread in Principle 8 (change and delivery). If we are going to measure our ability to deliver that steel thread, what are the critical success factors we need to have in place? They should be financial and focus on customers, internal processes and innovation. Once you identify the critical success factors, they will determine what needs to be done to improve and innovate to create value for customers and to continue to develop a competitive advantage. Those factors may be different

depending on your organisation and sector, but the categories will be the same. Deeper thinking is needed to decide what measurements matter. A good place to start is an outside-in view that the customer has.

Performance management

We need to determine somebody's performance based on the value they create rather than the amount of work they do. Unfortunately, our current structures were designed for the industrial age to get work through a production line rather than solve business problems. If we accept that we're in a knowledge age and knowledge and expertise are the currency that drives real value, then we must measure somebody's success based on the value that they create. To determine that value, you have to align it with a set of KPIs and be agnostic about the amount of work they do to deliver value. If they deliver 100 things but fail to hit those measures, then they should be deemed to have failed. If they deliver only one thing but achieve the outcome then they are a success and should be rewarded or recognised for that. It is not about the number of hours they put in or where they show up to work, it is about the value that they create for the organisation.

Performance management as it is currently done is fundamentally a broken process. People are given projects to do and rewarded for delivering them, but often there is no clear understanding of whether they are delivering real value that fulfils your strategy and benefits your customers. We advocate creating a true meritocracy in which your people are rewarded for the value they create rather than the amount of work they do. If the value is aligned with what matters to you most, your organisation will benefit and your people should share in that success. Work becomes purposeful and meaningful as opposed to transactional.

Eliyahu Goldratt, in *The Haystack Syndrome*, said, 'Tell me how you measure me, and I will tell you how

I behave.'[65] This is a great quote and we have seen it in action many times. The traditional performance management system prevalent in many organisations has been around for over 100 years since a time when people were managed by quotas of manual tasks of low cognitive burden (shovelling, bolting things together etc). Managers assumed employees were inherently lazy and set standardised ways of doing things and quotas. Interestingly, the humble Gantt chart was created at this time to track quotas of pig iron moved by individuals. We now use this deterministic tool to track £100 million projects. Nothing much from a management aspect has changed since that time. The underlying belief is that managing performance directly impacts output or outcome. For simple tasks, requiring little brain power, that's true – but it has been proven time and time again that traditional performance management (hit this number and you will get this financial bonus) causes adverse behaviours and worsens performance. Yet we still use it as a tool and many people expect it as part of the job.

Let's look at an example: a salesperson is incentivised to hit 100 widgets per year. They achieve that number in nine months and 'sandbag' further potential orders for next year as there is no monetary incentive for achieving over 100 sales. Their intention is to set themself up well for next year. If they overachieve, they will only be given a harder target next year. The adverse effects: variation in ordering cadence drives cost into the business (inventory and stockholding) resulting in shortages in January as 'peak' orders arrive and lost business opportunities in the last quarter of the year.

On top of this, sales are rarely a one-person game. They are usually a team game, yet sometimes we only reward some roles. It's like just paying the striker in a football team a bonus for every goal irrespective of whether the team wins or not. Imagine what that does for morale in the remainder of the team.

Performance is often benchmarked, creating a level of competition among colleagues. We have seen organisations that are proud of their focus on hiring the best people and then average and normalise performance along a bell curve. Often organisations can attract great talent but don't have the means to host it.

Those measurements, implemented with the best intentions, often drive behaviour in the wrong direction. An individual bonus might encourage people to be competitive rather than collaborative with their colleagues. Performance management should be directed at learning and development and fully decoupled from reward. The fairest way of thinking about reward is profit share. If we all win as a team, we all take a share of the spoils. If we lose as a team, why would some still win? Imagine the simplification of your performance management process and overhead.

Balancing metrics

Metrics cannot be done in isolation. Overdoing a metric in one part of the organisation could have an adverse effect somewhere else, therefore balancing metrics is essential. Chasing a number without thinking about the impact it might have elsewhere will have a detrimental effect on the customer.

Targets can drive adverse behaviours that weren't intended. There is an old saying that any manager can hit a target, even if they have to destroy the organisation to do so. The target will be gamed regardless of how we do it. A prime example of this was measuring average call handling time in call centres. They set a target of ninety seconds per call. When this was

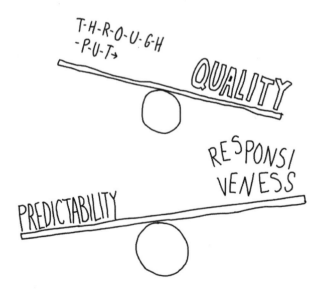

linked to performance assessments and reward, call staff simply put the phones down when they reached eighty-five seconds to hit their target. This led to a repeat call coming in somewhere else. With so many new calls coming in, they needed a new contact centre which drove costs up further. This is called failure demand. When you start to investigate and measure it in contact centres or delivery teams, you may see rates as high as 70% in some cases. That means 70% of the work the team does is because it wasn't done right the first time. It is easy to significantly improve this once we measure it and understand it. We need to be careful with targets and think instead about trends. It's important to understand what your metric is, whether you want a positive or a negative trend and then track the trend rather than setting an arbitrary target.

An organisation we worked with thought they were measuring productivity. On investigation, we found they were gauging productivity using a proxy by measuring how utilised their people were (>85%) and their conformance to an arbitrary plan. We encouraged them to look at different metrics – measuring productivity in terms of throughput, predictability, responsiveness and quality. Through investigation, study and experimentation, they agreed that if they could improve the trends in those areas, the organisation would be in a good place. The CFO asked what targets we should implement for year-end but we talked them out of doing that. We wanted the teams to continually improve and simply drive the trends in the right direction, allowing them to be innovative about how they did it. In reality, they were balancing metrics. If one metric was overdone, it would be seen in another metric being compromised. If they over-focused on throughput, quality would dip. If they overfocused on predictability, their responsiveness would dip. After nine months, the team had improved all four metrics, most significantly doubling through-put while halving the size of the team. This was a much better improvement than the CFO would have set as a target and demonstrated that good measures and empowered teams can work wonders. Doing more with less became a reality – a common dynamic we see with clients when they measure what matters.

CASE STUDY: STATISTICAL ANALYSIS AT A LARGE RETAILER

In a meeting with directors of a large UK retailer, the MD talked about a new store format they had been trialling in ten stores. They wanted to roll it out across 300 other stores at a cost of millions of pounds. It was proudly stated that the trial had shown a 3% improvement in the margin. We asked if this 3% was statistically significant. It became clear that the 3% was measured against a mean but no real analysis had been done. We were asked to analyse the data and found that the trial store results were not statistically different from the rest of the population of stores. There were differences but, from a statistical point of view, it was within the normal variation seen across the whole estate. They say there are 'lies, damn lies and statistics'.

Using data correctly stopped the rollout and saved millions of wasted pounds. Interestingly, the analysis also identified a store (that wasn't part of the trial) that was a positive statistical outlier. We suggested carrying out an in-depth analysis to identify what that store was doing to create a statistically significant increase in margin – and replicating that instead.

Summary

In any organisation, you need to measure the value you create, not the activities that you do. Work starts to feel meaningful and purposeful because people are delivering lasting value to a business. If you create reward structures that allow everybody to share in the success of the business, you will have an engaged workforce who buy into the purpose and mission of the company.

Beware of your experience and intuition around measurements. They are unreliable. Measure what matters to the customer. The quote, 'Not everything that counts can be counted, and not everything that can be counted counts,' is an important one to remember.[66] Unless you think like that, you'll become a slave to the numbers.

Targets can and will be gamed. Trends can be owned and improved by people using autonomy and innovation. Choose wisely.

Actions to take

1. Measure what matters to the customer.

2. Use balancing metrics to highlight when you are overdoing one area.

3. Decouple performance management from monetary reward or punishment and align it with learning.

4. Performance management using individual incentives and arbitrary targets often drives unwanted behaviours. Consider performance enablement at the team level.

Summary

We believe that you will see a positive impact on your organisation if you deploy the twelve principles of the Future Business Formula we have outlined in this book. They are evidenced through the case studies and Formula 1 examples. Let's bring all twelve principles together as a final reminder:

TWELVE PRINCIPLES	
Strategy	Create a strategy for an unpredictable world – emergent, adaptive, relevant.
Customer	Create experiences, the new differentiator.
Alignment	Embrace purpose and transparency; make action irresistible.
Leadership	Use influence to benefit others.

Culture	Be intentional about creating a positive culture.
Talent	Create the sought-after organisation to work in and work with.
Innovation	Leverage cognitive diversity; allow ideas to flourish.
Change and delivery	Focus on delivering small packets of value regularly.
Simplification	Operate at the speed of a start-up.
Organisational design	Embed an adaptive operating model.
Learning	Bring diverse opinions into the room.
Measurement	Measure what matters to the customer.

Every environment and organisation is unique and you will have to find your path through to make these principles work. As leaders, you can use this book as a guide and, through a discovery process, you will find the best way to apply them within your organisation. Start with the actions at the end of each chapter to get a foothold.

The theme throughout this book is that the business world is now demonstrating VUCA. The highly volatile, uncertain, complex and ambiguous world that we are in requires us to take a new emergent approach to be effective. The best way to lead through a complex environment is to follow principles and work it out as you experiment and learn, rather than following the paint-by-numbers, predesigned solution on a logical plan, despite its initial allure.

Technology

A section on technology may be conspicuous by its absence. We have not discussed technology intentionally as we believe it is rarely a true differentiator. With the digital revolution underway, technology has been democratised. Differentiation can be found in the way technology is used, especially in the customer experience layer. This is true in Formula 1 as it is in other industries. Any small advantage in technology can be quickly reeled back in by the competition.

The continuous journey

This is not about setting a vision, moving towards it and hoping you will be OK when you get there. This is a journey that never ends and requires continuous focus and effort to make progress in the right direction. It is not about the destination; it is about the journey. If the journey is in the right direction – you are following the principles, you believe that there's a better route and continuous improvement is at the core of what you do – you will get to a better place.

You should always pursue differentiation and the things that are going to give you a competitive edge and make you stand out from the crowd. If you stop doing that, you are on a slow death march or may even start going backwards. The competition will pass you by, the baseline will shift and your organisation will decline.

Call to action

We have built our experience and viewpoint on these twelve principles by observing what makes Formula 1 a special industry and helping organisations in different industries successfully apply these principles in the real world. It is a difficult journey to do alone, but there continue to be great successes when organisations apply these principles. It comes back to who this book is for. It needs leadership with a punk or pirate mentality – the people in an organisation who are willing to challenge the status quo and are comfortable exploring the unknown and taking risks. We believe it is these punks, pirates, mavericks and rebels – the ones who see things differently – who are critical for the future of business.

We believe in inspiring the future of work. There has to be a better future for the next generation. We are at an inflection point. The world is moving faster than ever before and human consciousness is growing with each generation. Customers and technology are changing. How we do business and build organisations hasn't kept up. What worked in a bygone age is no longer useful. These twelve principles are a distillation of a Future Business Formula.

ADRIAN STALHAM   MARK GALLAGHER

References

1   FW Taylor, *The Principles of Scientific Management* (Harper & Brothers, 1911)
2   J Harter, 'Historic drop in employee engagement follows record rise', Gallup Workplace (2 July 2020), www.gallup.com/workplace/313313/historic-drop-employee-engagement-follows-record-rise.aspx, accessed 9 December 2022
3   S Sorensen, 'How employee engagement drives growth', Gallup Workplace (20 June 2013), www.gallup.com/workplace/236927/employee-engagement-drives-growth.aspx, accessed 9 December 2022
4   K Beck et al. 'The Agile Manifesto', Agile Alliance (2001), www.agilealliance.org/agile101/the-agile-manifesto, accessed 9 December 2022

5 'Age and tenure in the C-Suite', Korn Ferry (2019), www.kornferry.com/about-us/press/age-and-tenure-in-the-c-suite, accessed 3 May 2022

6 Interview with Neil Martin, 13 May 2020

7 A Ovans, 'What is strategy, again?', *Harvard Business Review* (12 May 2015), https://hbr.org/2015/05/what-is-strategy-again,

8 A Ali, 'Powering the internet and Amazon's profits', Visual Capitalist (10 July 2022), www.visualcapitalist.com/aws-powering-the-internet-and-amazons-profits, accessed 9 December 2022

9 'Why F1 chooses AWS', AWS (no date), https://aws.amazon.com/sports/f1, accessed 9 December 2022

10 'Formula 1 Virtual Grand Prix series achieves record-breaking viewership', Formula 1 (19 June 2020), www.formula1.com/en/latest/article.formula-1-virtual-grand-prix-series-achieves-record-breaking-viewership.7bv94UJPCtxW0L5mwTxBHk.html, accessed 9 December 2022

11 'Formula 1 Virtual Grand Prix series achieves record-breaking viewership', Formula 1 (19 June 2020), www.formula1.com/en/latest/article.formula-1-virtual-grand-prix-series-achieves-record-breaking-viewership.7bv94UJPCtxW0L5mwTxBHk.html, accessed 9 December 2022

12 D-M Davis, 'Gen Zers have a spending power of over $140 billion, and it's driving the frenzy of retailers and brands trying to win their dollars', *Insider* (28 January 2020), www.businessinsider.

com/retail-courts-gen-z-spending-power-over-140-billion-2020-1?r=US&IR=T, accessed 9 December 2022

13 'Millennials: Fuelling the experience economy', Eventbrite (survey conducted by Harris Poll), 2014, https://eventbrite-s3.s3.amazonaws.com/marketing/Millennials_Research/Gen_PR_Final.pdf, accessed 9 December 2022

14 S Pandolph, 'Instagram is highly influential in style purchases', *Insider* (30 August 2017), www.businessinsider.com/instagram-is-highly-influential-in-style-purchases-2017-8?r=US&IR=T, accessed 9 December 2022

15 A Abad-Santos, 'Nike's Colin Kaepernick ad sparked a boycott — and earned $6 billion for Nike', *Vox* (24 September 2018), www.vox.com/2018/9/24/17895704/nike-colin-kaepernick-boycott-6-billion, accessed 9 December 2022

16 'Facebook to acquire Oculus', Meta (25 March 2014), https://about.fb.com/news/2014/03/facebook-to-acquire-oculus, accessed 9 December 2022

17 *The 2019 Feature Adoption Report*, Pendo (2019), www.pendo.io/resources/the-2019-feature-adoption-report, accessed 9 December 2022

18 M Syed, *Black Box Thinking: The surprising truth about success* (John Murray, 2015)

19 G Anderson, 'F1's last entry by US car giant was a masterclass in failure', *The Race* (8 January 2023), https://the-race.com/formula-1/ford-

jaguar-failed-team-us-manufacturer, accessed
12 December 2022

20 D Coulthard, *The Winning Formula: Leadership,
strategy and motivation the F1 way* (Blink
Publishing, 2018)

21 G Anderson, 'Why Jaguar was a masterclass in
how to get F1 wrong', *The Race* (30 March 2020),
https://the-race.com/formula-1/why-jaguar-
was-a-masterclass-in-how-to-get-f1-wrong,
accessed 12 December 2022

22 A Newey, *How to Build a Car: The autobiography
of the world's greatest Formula 1 designer* (Harper
Collins, 2017)

23 A Newey, *How to Build a Car*

24 'Should've been mega: Toyota in F1', *The Race*
(5 May 2020), https://the-race.com/formula-1/
shouldve-been-mega-toyota-in-f1, accessed
12 December 2022

25 M Gascoyne, Lecture for Performance Insights
Ltd, London Business School (2016)

26 T Wolff, 'Leadership styles, finding purpose and no
blame culture in F1', Mercedes AMG Petronas
Formula One Team Deep Dive series, YouTube
(16 April 2020), www.youtube.com/watch?v=
q8mGymE7bXo, accessed 12 December 2022

27 T Wolff, 'Leadership styles, finding purpose and no
blame culture in F1', Mercedes AMG Petronas
Formula One Team Deep Dive series, YouTube
(16 April 2020), www.youtube.com/watch?v=
q8mGymE7bXo, accessed 12 December 2022

28 K Schwab, 'The Fourth Industrial Revolution: What it means, how to respond', World Economic Forum (4 January 2016), www.weforum.org/agenda/2016/01/the-fourth-industrial-revolution-what-it-means-and-how-to-respond, accessed 12 December 2022

29 JB Watson, *Psychological Care of Infant and Child* (WW Norton Company, 1928)

30 RK Greenleaf, *The Servant as Leader* (The Greenleaf Center for Servant Leadership, 2012)

31 S Bahcall, *Loonshots: How to nurture the crazy ideas that win wars, cure diseases, and transform industries* (St Martin's Press, 2019)

32 'F1 Esports series presented by Aramco returns remotely for fourth series with record prize fund', Formula1.com (13 August 2020), https://corp.formula1.com/f1-esports-series-presented-by-aramco-returns-remotely-for-fourth-season-with-record-prize-fund, accessed 12 December 2022

33 A Newey, *How to Build a Car*

34 A Newey, *How to Build a Car*

35 Interview with Mark Gallagher for At The Controls podcast, 5 November 2020

36 S Pleiter, 'Engaging employees', *Smith Magazine* (winter 2014), https://smith.queensu.ca/magazine/issues/winter-2014/features/engaging-employees.php, accessed 12 December 2022

37 E Schein, *Organizational Culture and Leadership*, 5th Edition (Wiley, 2017)

38 V Hunt, D Layton and S Prince, 'Why diversity matters', McKinsey & Company (January 2015), www.mckinsey.com/~/media/mckinsey/ business%20functions/people%20and%20 organizational%20performance/our%20 insights/why%20diversity%20matters/why%20 diversity%20matters.pdf, accessed 12 December 2022

39 M Syed, *Rebel Ideas: The power of diverse thinking* (John Murray, 2019)

40 C Warren, 'Here's why Apple is flying a pirate flag to celebrate its 40th anniversary', *Mashable* (1 April 2016), https://mashable.com/article/ apple-pirate-flag-40th-anniversary, accessed 12 December 2022

41 A Newey, *How to Build a Car*

42 A Newey, *How to Build a Car*

43 RD Stacey, *Complexity and Creativity in Organizations* (Berrett-Koehler Publishers, 1996)

44 D Snowden, 'Liberating Knowledge' opening chapter in *Liberating Knowledge CBI Business Guide* (Caspian Publishing, 1999)

45 R Ackoff, Systems thinking speech, YouTube (2 November 2015), www.youtube.com/ watch?v=EbLh7rZ3rhU

46 K Beck et al. 'The Agile Manifesto', Agile Alliance (2001), www.agilealliance.org/agile101/ the-agile-manifesto, accessed 9 December 2022

47 K Beck et al. 'The Agile Manifesto', Agile Alliance (2001), www.agilealliance.org/ agile101/the-agile-manifesto, accessed 9 December 2022

48 M Gascoyne, Lecture for Performance Insights
    Ltd, London Business School (2016)

49 CN Parkinson, 'Parkinson's Law', *The Economist*
    (19 November 1955)

50 M Weber, *The Theory of Social and Economic
    Organization* (Free Press, 1947)

51 G Hamel and M Zanini, *Humanocracy: Creating
    organizations as amazing as the people inside them*
    (Harvard Business Review Press, 2020)

52 B Bogsnes, 'The end of performance
    management', YouTube (5 November 2019),
    www.youtube.com/watch?v=SC6CFOx1WQc

53 'Should've been mega: Toyota in F1', *The Race*
    (5 May 2020), https://the-race.com/formula-1/
    shouldve-been-mega-toyota-in-f1, accessed
    12 December 2022

54 'Toyota – 5 Core Values', LeanVlog, YouTube (nd),
    www.youtube.com/watch?v=91hXhqgRGNM

55 M Gallagher, 'Toyota in F1', *GP Racing*
    (January 2021)

56 M Gallagher, 'Toyota in F1', *GP Racing*
    (January 2021)

57 FW Taylor, *The Principles of Scientific Management*
    (Harper & Brothers, 1911)

58 N Pflaeging, *Organize for Complexity: How to get
    life back into work to build the high-performance
    organization* (BetaCodex Publishing, 2014)

59 T Boon, 'Was selling low-cost carrier "Go" BA's
    greatest mistake?', *Simple Flying* (26 September
    2018), https://simpleflying.com/british-
    airways-go, accessed 15 December 2022

60 RIM Dunbar, 'Neocortex size as a constraint on group size in primates', *Journal of Human Evolution* (1992), 22 (6): 469–493

61 *Formula 1: Drive to Survive*, Series 2, Episode 4, Netflix (2020)

62 D Coulthard, *The Winning Formula*

63 D Coulthard, *The Winning Formula*

64 J Estrin, 'Kodak's first digital moment', *The New York Times* (12 August 2015), https://lens.blogs.nytimes.com/2015/08/12/kodaks-first-digital-moment, accessed 16 December 2022

65 EM Goldratt, *The Haystack Syndrome: Sifting information out of the data ocean* (North River Press, 1990)

66 The origins of this quote are disputed. It has been misattributed to Albert Einstein but is likely by William Bruce Cameron: WB Cameron, *Informal Sociology: A causal introduction to sociological thinking* (Random House, 1963)

Acknowledgements

Adrian Stalham: I would like to thank the following people who have made this book possible through their support and contributions:

Pat Lynes, for your patient persistence, guidance and encouragement that helped me find my place and voice over the many years we have known each other. Your positivity and contribution to the process of creating this book is greatly appreciated.

Darren Linden, for your insightful knowledge and dedication to transformation that helped refine the content of this book. Your guidance and advice have been invaluable.

Jacqueline Shakespeare, for your encouragement and motivation throughout the writing process. Your belief in me and this project has been a source of inspiration.

I would also like to extend my thanks to all those who have supported me in this endeavour, including my family, friends and colleagues at Sullivan & Stanley. Your encouragement and confidence in me made the difference during the more difficult days.

Additionally, a special thanks to the clients I have had the privilege of working with over the years. Your trust and confidence provided me with the opportunities to test my ideas and deliver value for you and your organisations. I am grateful for the experiences we have shared and the lessons we learned along the way.

Mark Gallagher: I would like to thank principal author Adrian Stalham for his help, support and guidance in producing this book. Also Pat Lynes and Jacqueline Shakespeare at Sullivan & Stanley for their valuable insights and support. My thanks to interviewees from the *At The Controls* podcast, including Neil Martin from Paceteq, James Allison, Holly Chapman and Bradley Lord from the Mercedes-AMG Petronas F1 team and Mike Gascoyne of MGI Engineering. Also to podcast host Jonathan Legard. Thanks too are due to both David Coulthard and Allan McNish for their insights and to Mika Häkkinen for kindly providing the Foreword to this book. Finally, thanks are due to Debbie Price and Jill McLachlan from Performance Insights for their brilliant work and support during the writing of this book.

The Authors

 **Adrian Stalham** is the Chief Change Officer at Sullivan & Stanley, an award-winning change consultancy. His career started in immunodiagnostic R&D for infectious diseases such as hepatitis at Johnson & Johnson where he first found his penchant for project management and problem-solving. In his part-time job as a bouncer at nightclubs and bars, he discovered a keen interest in human behaviour and psychology. These foundations sparked a long change and transformation career across many large companies and a variety of industries. Adrian is happiest with a whiteboard and a set

of Post-its, collaborating with a diverse group on the solution to a problem.

 **Mark Gallagher** is Managing Director of Performance Insights, providing companies with the opportunity to learn from the fast-paced business environment of Formula 1 motor racing, an arena in which leading teams embrace change and use it to derive competitive advantage. Mark's career has included being a member of the management board of two well-known Formula 1 teams – Jordan Grand Prix (now Aston Martin F1) and Red Bull Racing – as well as bringing famed engine supplier Cosworth back into the sport in 2010. Mark has been a professional public speaker on business topics relating to Formula 1 for over twenty years, delivering insights to more than 800 companies spanning a diverse range of industrial and business sectors.

You can contact us on:

🌐 www.sullivanstanley.com

🐦 @sullyandstan
www.twitter.com/sullyandstan

📷 www.instagram.com/sullyandstan

Adrian Stalham

in Adrian Stalham
www.linkedin.com/in/adrian-stalham-97a6513

Mark Gallagher

🌐 www.performanceinsights.co.uk

in www.linkedin.com/in/markgallagherf1

🐦 @_markgallagher
https://twitter.com/_markgallagher?lang=en

📷 @_markgallagher
www.instagram.com/_markgallagher/?hl=en